...and
death
came third!

GW01007081

...and death came third!

Andy Lopata and Peter Roper

First Published In Great Britain 2006
by www.BookShaker.com

© Copyright Andy Lopata & Peter Roper

All rights reserved. No part of this publication may be reproduced, stored in or introduced into a retrieval system, or transmitted, in any form, or by any means (electronic, mechanical, photocopying recording or otherwise) without the prior written permission of the publisher.

This book is sold subject to the condition that it shall not, by way of trade or otherwise, be lent, resold, hired out, or otherwise circulated without the publisher's prior consent in any form of binding or cover other than that in which it is published and without a similar condition including this condition being imposed on the subsequent purchaser.

Typeset in Century Schoolbook

Praise For This Book

"A must–read for anyone who wants to get on in business."

Sir Digby Jones, Director–General of the CBI, www.cbi.org.uk

"The one book on networking and presenting I'd have if I could have just one. Excellent!"

Thomas Power, Chairman of Ecademy and author, 'Networking for Life', www.ecademy.com

"This book belongs in the collection of every self respecting professional speaker."

Nigel Risner, Author, 'The Impact Code', Speaker of the year from both The Academy of Chief Executives and TEC 2005, www.nigelrisner.com

"A very readable, practical and yet well humoured guide to networking/presenting. It's the kind of book that should be close by day to day, because it gives you punchy reminders and summaries that help to keep you sharp and focused. I've placed an order for every one of my team because every one of us can take something from it and build on our existing skills."

Andy Moss, Senior Business Development Manager, Lloyds TSB, www.lloydstsb.co.uk

"Anyone who's ever wanted to be able to network confidently can benefit from the down–to–earth knowledge in this book."

Mike Southon, Co–author, 'The Beermat Entrepreneur', www.beermat.biz

"An excellent guide to networking and speaking with confidence. Apply Peter's and Andy's knowledge and you'll feel much more self–assured in front of others."

Brendan Power, Founder and Past President, Professional Speakers Association, www.BrendanPower.com, www.professionalspeakers.org

"Powerful, practical advice on both cultivating great networking relationships and speaking with confidence; two skills of vital importance to today's successful business person. Utilize the wisdom in this book and watch your bank account grow while you enjoy your work more and more."

Bob Burg, Author, 'Endless Referrals: Network Your Everyday Contacts into Sales', www.burg.com

"Those of you that want to make something quickly from your life and career should consider this book as a "Start UP" book. It's a simple straightforward read with lots of tips and tools. It's comprehensive and easy to read and is full of anecdotes. Great value."

Brian Chernett, Founder, The Academy for Chief Executives, www.chiefexecutive.com

"As a how–to guide, this book contains everything you may need to know. Brimming with straightforward strategies anyone can use to overcome the key fears associated with networking and presenting."

David Attwood, Joint Managing Director, Start–Rite Shoes Ltd, www.start–rite.co.uk

"Here is a fantastic book of tips, tactics and approaches that simply work."

Terry Forrester, Managing Director, Initiatives in Business Development (ibd) Group Ltd, www.ibd–uk.com

"What I like most about the book is that the principles and concepts about networking are honest and open. As someone who knows a little about networking myself, I believe I am qualified to say this without fear of contradiction."

Will Kintish, Leading UK authority on networking for the professional and financial communities, www.kintish.co.uk

"This easy to read style is a great introduction for anyone wanting to network."

Etta Cohen, Founder, Forward Ladies, www.forwardladies.com

"'...and death came third!' cuts straight to the chase on what you need to do to make the most of the opportunities that come your way."

Julia Lea, National President Junior Chamber of Commerce International UK 2005, www.jciuk.org.uk

"The information within these pages could be your very own acres of diamonds. It's rare to find such honest advice in such an accessible format. This book is surely destined to become a classic."

David Hyner, International speaker, trainer and researcher, www.davidhyner.com, www.stretchdevelopment.com

"What an outstanding reference book! The pages are quite simply saturated with wisdom and full of practical tips that will get you the great results you desire. If you only ever buy one volume on speaking and networking, make sure it is '...and death came third!'"

Tony Burgess, Director, Academy of High Achievers (Aha!), www.aha-success.com

"Our body needs feeding when hungry or we die; our potential to survive and prosper in business is directly fed by our ability to 'network and speak' effectively in public – read this book, feed it into your mind and then take action, if you want to survive!"

Reg Athwal, Entrepreneur, Best-selling Author of 'Wake Up and Live the Life You Love' and 'RAW Questions series', www.regathwal.com

"Many clients tell me they simply dread the presenting and networking they have to do as part of their roles. Anybody who has ever wanted to network or speak confidently can benefit from the down-to-earth knowledge in this book."

Lesley Everett, Personal Branding Coach and author of Walking TALL, www.walkingtall.org

"Successful networking depends upon your ability to make other people as passionate about what you do as you are, this gem of a book shows you how."
Andrew Clark, The Speakers' Academy, www.speakers-academy.com

"Networking is a skill that has to be learnt and absorbed until it becomes integral to all people in everything that they do. Students should learn this from the very beginning and should enter the workplace knowing how to put relationships before commerce. If you are already in business, or if you are a student, this book is a must read."
Penny Power, Founder of Ecademy, www.ecademy.com

"This book is a great reminder that you can never stop networking. I discovered new ways of networking and, for people new to networking, reading the book could make a big difference to their business."
Tim Kidson, Co-author of 'Pylgrim's Progress: How to be a WINNER in the Global Knowledge Economy', www.growth-for-business.com

"In these days of email, voice mail and all the other mails, there is a danger that we may forget how to communicate directly and effectively with people. Andy's book is a timely reminder of the importance of strong personal interaction in business. An indispensable tool for any networker, or would-be networker."
David Jordan, Speakeasy, www.speakeasy.gb.com

"If you're looking to truly understand how to maximise the results you get from any networking opportunity – then look no further. Andy's and Peter's book presents all the ideas you need"
Peter Thomson. Peter Thomson International plc, www.peterthomson.com

"The ability to express yourself clearly is vital in networking & public speaking. The down–to–earth knowledge in this book shows you that you can be a great communicator by being yourself and you don't need tricks or to hide behind your business."

Dave Clarke, CEO of NRG Business Networks, www.nrg–networks.com

"When you apply the insights and tips in this book you will never have to fear another networking event or presentation. So please don't only read this book, but also put its wisdom into practice. Your life WILL be different!"

Jan Vermeiren, Networking Coach and author of 'Let's Connect!', www.networking–coach.com

"This is a book full of powerful and practical strategies and techniques to help you overcome shyness, present yourself confidently and effectively so that you can make the most of your networking. Full of real life examples that bring the theory alive, the book shows you exactly what you need to do to make the most of opportunities that come your way."

Dawn Charles, Managing Director, The Women's Retreat, www.thewomensretreat.co.uk, Director, A Woman's Place, www.awp.ecademy.com

"The Manufacturing Foundation has conducted a number of research projects to examine the bases for success in a wide cross–section of manufacturing businesses and in the development of their leaders. In each case networking is identified as a key tool for this success. Packed with anecdotes that bring the subject vividly to life, this book provides powerful, practical and solid advice on networking and speaking with confidence. Anyone who's ever wanted to be able to network / speak confidently can benefit from the down–to–earth knowledge that this book provides."

Clive Boast, Special Advisor, The Manufacturing Foundation, www.manufacturingfoundation.co.uk

"In my role as Canary Wharf Group plc's Local Business Liaison Manager and, until 2003, as Chairwoman of the Women in Docklands Network, I have been networking and encouraging others to do so for the past ten years. This book is not only a good read; it is well structured and has also given me a lot of useful tips."

Gay Harrington, Canary Wharf Group plc,
www.canarywharfcommunityoutreach.com

"I particularly liked the easy style of writing – you talked to me straight out of the book! Very 'been there and done that', which inspires confidence to go on and try all the various tips provided. Networking is an essential part of successful business in today's world and in this book you've armed the reader with everything anyone could need to succeed."

Jackie Groundsell, The Women's Company,
www.thewomenscompany.com

"I met Andy two years ago, and have had a string of referrals from him. This book shows how he does it – and why he gets such fun from building up mutually productive relationships."

Peter Griffiths, Author, 'The Economist's Tale',
www.griffithsspeaker.com

"This is the book to learn how to be the best networker – full of tips, tools and techniques with real examples to support the key messages. Practise what you read and you will see a noticeable difference in your personal and professional life."

Carole McKellar, Managing Director, Resources for Business,
Association and Event Specialist, www.rfb.co.uk

"This book bursts with passion. Filled with commonsense advice and packed with timely anecdotes, this book will inspire you; I guarantee it. Opened at random, virtually every page revealed something new or reminded me of something useful that I had forgotten. Whether you come to it as a novice or a seasoned campaigner you will find an abundance of great ideas couched in straightforward language. A gem of a book."

Jim Ewan, Past President, Professional Speakers Association, www.JimEwan.com, www.professionalspeakers.org

"Let's cut to the chase, here is THE Handbook on all the network and presenting skills you need. However long you've been going to such meetings or doing presentations, the opportunity to refresh your tactics and be stimulated by new ideas is one not to be missed."

Hilary Hall, Chief Executive, The Midland Association of Restaurants, Caterers, Hotels & Entertainment Sector, www.marchassc.org.uk

"The tips in this book made me well over £1,000,000!

'...and death came third!' contains a practical, hands on and (very refreshing) common sense approach to applying networking to your business – the value of which cannot be underestimated!

You never know when you'll meet that one special contact who could so dramatically impact your business you won't even recognise it... so you'd better be ready... Ready or Not... READ THIS BOOK. The tips and techniques outlined in this book led me to meet people that transformed me from an inwardly thinking, single dimension business person... to an outward thinking, multi dimensional, all round entrepreneur, investor and educator."

Sunil Jaiswal, Entrepreneur, Investor & Educator, www.suniljaiswal.com

"Anyone who's ever wanted to be able to network/speak confidently can benefit from the down–to–earth knowledge in this book. I know I will be using it time after time as it is a powerhouse book of tips and tactics. I'll be recommending it to all my colleagues."

Helen Thomas, Managing Director, Westons Cider, www.westons–cider.co.uk

"This book is full of good things. I particularly liked the section on how actually to go about opening a conversation and building rapport. And the real–life examples work really well. It is an excellent read from which I am definitely going to benefit myself."

Adam Jolly, Editor of the Growing Business Handbook published by Kogan Page in association with the Institute of Directors www.kogan–page.co.uk

Peter and Andy are keen supporters of Speakers4Africa

A note from the founder: *"It is a privilege to be associated with two leading thinkers in the closely coupled worlds of networking and speaking. They also happen to be fellow members of the Professional Speakers Association and participants in the Speakers4Africa initiative where a world–wide community of speakers offer their time to speak in the business world and allow their fees from selected engagements to go in full to support charities benefiting needy communities in Africa. These are two men who "walk the talk" in a spirit of abundance. I wish them every success with this book."*

Clive Wilson, Founder, Speakers4Africa, www.speakers4africa.org

Acknowledgements

This book has been nearly two years in the writing as we have developed our ideas through many '...and death came third!' joint presentations, discussions and the gathering of more and more experiences for us to share with you. Naturally, there are a number of people to thank who helped get us to this point.

You cannot underestimate the importance of a good editor in the writing process, particularly where there is more than one author. Lesley Morrisey and Jo Parfitt at Summertime have done sterling work and we could not have found anyone better. Thanks as well to Annabel Crawford and Cindy–Michelle Waterfield for their invaluable contributions.

The enthusiastic team at Bookshaker.com, our publishers, have also raised our spirits and aspirations and we look forward to working closely with Debs and Joe on this project.

Stuart Townsend, our cover designer, has shown his brilliance once again.

We have learnt through our experience as Speakers that people love to hear stories and this book is full of them. Thanks to the many members of the Professional Speakers Association, BRE, Ecademy and our other networking contacts who have allowed us to use their stories to illustrate the many points made in the book.

Andy would particularly like to thank his family and his colleagues at BRE, both at Head Office and the Regional Partners, for their support. Peter's appreciation and love goes to his Mother, his children, Hazel, Sara–Beth and Chris for allowing us to use their stories. And most of all, to his wife Anny for her never–ending love and support.

Contents

Foreword

The need for 'networking' or 'presentation skills' did not enter my mind when I first started on my career path. Back then in the 80s they were not even considered to be key skills. Instinctively, I have always focused on making my mark, building connections and getting the message across to my listeners no matter how complex or challenging the issue. But it is only when I look back at the years I spent in huge corporations like Ernst & Young, Lloyds TSB and AXA Insurance, that I can begin to recognise just how important these skills truly are. In short, they were responsible for my success.

As you begin to achieve greater responsibility in a business environment, the need to be able to connect with others around you and to be able to present your information in a coherent and appealing way increases. You start to be asked to represent your company at meetings attended only by strangers and are expected to create rapport and make alliances. From time to time, as you continue to progress, you have to stand–up in front of a group or a conference and present your ideas. In all, the higher you climb the more your success depends on your ability to communicate effectively.

In business we all get faced with these situations – sometimes all at once! It took me many years of trial and error before I could claim to be an effective presenter and networker. I am delighted to find that two experts in their fields have joined forces to provide the definitive 'handbook' to help those people who still 'shake in their boots' at the thought of opening their mouths in the company of strangers.

Andy Lopata and Peter Roper are the experts from whom we should learn. Both are experienced and accomplished presenters and networkers and are both active in a number of business networks. In addition they are in demand as keynote speakers and present their topics at forums, workshops and conferences on a regular basis. In '...and death came third!', their knowledge and experience leaps off the page as they approach these two important subjects in a straightforward and accessible way, giving practical tips, expert guidance and easy–to–use tools.

This is the equivalent of a 'leg up' on the corporate ladder. I'm sure that the information contained in these pages will be invaluable in building your business success and your reputation.

I only wish that there had been something like this at the beginning of my career!

Peter Hubbard
Chief Executive, AXA Insurance

Introduction

In 1984 a New York Times study on Social Anxiety asked people what they most feared. Death came third. The top two fears were walking into a room of strangers and speaking in public.

Andy Lopata and Peter Roper came together because they do for a living what most people are afraid of – Andy is a professional networker and a director of a networking organisation, Business Referral Exchange; whilst Peter is a professional speaker.

Andy says, "I must be one of the luckiest people alive. I know that I am one of the luckiest people in the working population.

"The reason why I am so lucky is that I absolutely love my job; I thoroughly enjoy what I do. I go out and meet new people all the time; I learn about business; I learn about people.

"Through meeting people, learning about their business and discussing their concerns, their experiences and their thoughts, I get new ideas. This benefits both me and my business. For ideas like these you would have to pay consultants thousands of pounds.

"This is a two way street – while I am enjoying myself I find opportunities to help other people as well. One of the things that gives me the biggest buzz is helping other people – I get a thrill when I see their successes as a result.

"I get all of this because my business is networking, and that's what I love."

Peter has enormous enthusiasm for speaking, but recognises that it isn't everyone's natural element.

"Why do I talk, consult and write about speaking? I'm passionate about it, that's why!

"I firmly believe that it is a fundamental business requirement. If you're in business in some form or another, eventually you will need to speak professionally about your business and about what you do.

"This might be at a Chamber of Commerce event, a networking breakfast, lunch or dinner or simply when someone asks you "What do you do?"

"How well do you respond to a simple question like that? Have you got a well polished and carefully thought out answer, or do you find yourself struggling to express yourself in a way that is interesting?

"I don't believe you have to be a natural orator. I just mean that you can speak in a way that is comfortable for you and in a way that gets your message across.

"Being able to explain clearly and concisely what you do in a way that is engaging is the first step to promoting your business or your skills. Once you have done this a few times you'll find that people want you to get up and tell the assembled people more about your business – even a one minute presentation is a challenge for most people."

I'm sure that you've heard the phrase 'working the room'. Andy will help you make the room work for you. While Peter will ensure that, if you do stand up and speak about your business or expertise as often as possible, you will start to become known as an expert in your field. It's a great way to market your business.

This book is designed to help you to succeed by helping you to understand how to network to benefit you and your business.

THE ART OF NETWORKING

The tips, tools & techniques to help you network with confidence

What Is 'Networking'?

"Networking shouldn't be a hit and miss affair, businesses need to actively seek out opportunities where they can meet and mix with others in the business world. As well as being highly motivational, these kind of events throw up contacts and ideas that can significantly boost your business potential."

Sir Digby Jones, Director General, Confederation of British Industry speaking at IBN in Sheffield in February 2005

Networking occurs everywhere, as a part of everyday life. From parents at the school gates exchanging contacts, local knowledge and asking for help while waiting for their children to emerge, to businessmen discussing their companies after a game of golf. It has been around since the dawn of time and it is only in recent years that networking groups have sprung up *en masse* with a clear business focus. Networking isn't about groups and organisations, they merely facilitate it. Networking is, and should be, about people – and it should occur naturally.

As Carol Harris says in her book *Networking for Success*, "People are *the* essential element in today's business world. In past times, bricks and mortar, machinery, equipment and money were the major resources; nowadays we increasingly come across terms such as knowledge management, intellectual capital and relationship management."

Yet still many people turn their back on networking. Marketing consultants and agencies discuss it as a business strategy much less frequently with their clients than advertising and PR campaigns; businesses turn their noses up at invitations comparing events to Masonic Clubs or the 'Old School Tie', while others worry about being hunted down as sales fodder at such events.

Some people have approached networking from the wrong direction in the past, but I have seen many changes over recent years that suggest that networking is maturing as a business tool.

No longer do people go to such events to 'hunt', or certainly fewer people do.

This change was surely due. It is a fallacy to see man in his traditional role as 'The Hunter'. The truth is that, if the human race had relied on hunting for survival, we would probably be extinct by now. We are not naturally equipped to hunt; we did not have the necessary speed, strength, sense of smell or the claws and teeth to emerge victorious against other large species. Only by working together and using our minds to develop tools and strategies to survive could we thrive.

For the majority of our existence, man has been a farmer. We found that, by domesticating animals, they could provide us with both milk and meat without us needing to track and chase them down. We have nurtured and fed our livestock so that they could produce enough food and drink to satisfy our cravings. We harvested crops to supplement our diet. We have prospered the most where we have given back to the environment, planting new seeds, building shelters, looking after our livestock and rotating our crops.

Why then, do we approach our business contacts by hunting, looking for the quick kill? The traditional routes to marketing our business tend to focus on targeting prospective customers with the 'close' or the sale in mind. Cold calling is the prime example of this, with techniques taught to help salesmen lure their prospects to a point where they are bound to sign a contract.

More and more people now recognise the growing importance of 'word of mouth' marketing as a positive alternative. The focus is on attending networking events to build their business.

However, the first instinct for many when walking into a networking event has always been to be looking for potential customers, the people who will buy from us. On the other hand, experience tells us that nothing is more off–putting than somebody trying to sell to us without finding out about us first and ascertaining whether we truly need what they have to offer.

I remember attending a networking event in Liverpool a few years ago. As soon as I walked through the door, I was met by a member of the group hosting the event. Upon introducing myself, he thrust a business card into my hands and proceeded to tell me all about his business and its benefits.

What he didn't know, because he had not taken the time to find out, is that I was already a customer of theirs! Salespeople call it 'research'.

Many people, myself included, take advantage of the opportunity to block cold calls to our domestic telephone lines. Junk mail is often binned before being opened and advertising breaks on television are used as an opportunity to make a drink. If we don't like to be sold to, then why do we think that we should sell to others?

In accordance with man's natural skills, the most successful networkers are farmers, the people who go along to events to develop and nurture relationships. They are people who collect business cards from those they have made real contact with rather than hand their own cards out to anyone they meet. They are people who build a network of contacts whom they will support and who will support them in return.

And the good news is that there are more and more 'farmers' than 'hunters' now, certainly at the events I have attended recently. The shift in approach to networking over the last five years has been marked.

Networking is not about competing with others to see who can come out on top and claim the kill. It is about working together for the common good. Jan Vermeiren, in his book *Let's Connect*, offers an excellent summary of the difference between networking and selling:

"In a sales process the goal of the interaction between two people is the sale of a product or service. When networking, this sale could be the consequence of a contact that is built with respect and care. So it is clear that the sale is not the goal of networking, but a welcome and, in many cases, logical consequence."

Networking is about connecting. Networking is about enhancing your own individual potential by sharing knowledge, ideas and resources with others.

Go along to networking meetings and share your ideas with people there. Have a look at web–based networking forums, such as Ecademy, Ryze or LinkedIn, where members are constantly asking for advice, connections and new ideas. See how much people are prepared to help each other. Ask yourself how much time, effort and failure would have to be endured, without that support, by doing things on your own.

Many people who take advantage of networking opportunities are owners of small businesses. Across the world people are leaving multinational corporations, either through choice or because of downsizing, and are setting up their own businesses. A high proportion of these work on their own.

I have met many small business people who network more to get out of their own 'cave' than for new leads. One member of one of the Business Referral Exchange (BRE) weekly breakfast networking groups ran an Alfa–Romeo service centre. He did not need referrals; new business would come to him through Alfa dealerships, magazines and clubs.

He told me that he was networking because, day in and day out he found himself working just with his team of mechanics, people who either didn't understand or didn't care about the frustrations of running the business.

At networking events he could interact with people who shared the same joys, the same frustrations. Basically the same experiences. And he could rely on their support and encouragement.

When you hear people talk about networking, and they perceive that it is all about selling, selling and selling, you know that they haven't grasped how networking can help them to grow their businesses. Enhanced sales are not the be all and end all of networking; they are one of the benefits that can be gained from networking effectively.

Networking is the exchange of information. People help and support each other and, through that process, enhance each other's potential.

I will give you three tips, three tools and three techniques to help you network with confidence. If you really know what you want to achieve these will help you to get there. There is nothing in these pages that you do not already know, however, it is always good to refocus yourself on what you should be doing.

"Most people don't need to be taught,
they need only to be reminded."
C.S. Lewis

THREE TIPS

TIP 1 – Be Courageous

"It is not because things are difficult that we do not dare; it is because we do not dare that things are difficult."
Seneca

FEAR OF REJECTION

Why are we so frightened of meeting new people? Personally, I blame my mum! Throughout my childhood years my mother always used to warn me, "Don't talk to strangers!"

This childhood fear of strangers is very powerful, especially when combined with a fear of humiliation or rejection. Whenever we are put into a position where we are expected to meet new people, the adrenaline starts to flow and the nerves kick in.

It may make perfect sense to tell a young child to avoid strangers, but why do we carry this fear into adulthood? The situations faced by children and adults are very different and this advice is certainly redundant in most business or social engagements as an adult.

When was the last time that you went to a networking event and saw someone either being humiliated or being rejected?

Have you ever introduced yourself to someone to be met with a scowl and a barbed remark asking, "Who do you think you are?"

Have all the people in the room ever turned around and laughed at you for having the audacity to want to speak to someone you haven't met before?

It's very unlikely that any of these have happened to you at a networking event. After all, people attend these events because they want to meet new people.

Yes, there is a chance that our ego may be damaged if someone we approach shows no interest in us. But we can just dust ourselves off, move away and make it their problem, not ours. After all, they've missed out on the pleasure of getting to know us!

So the first tip is to *be courageous*. Swallow that fear. I know that this is easier said than done. Just remind yourself that most people share the same fear, including experienced networkers like me. I network for a living, I network everywhere, I love talking to strangers, but I still don't like that feeling of walking into a room where I don't know anyone. I just have to remind myself why I am there and why everyone else is there and, once I have started my first conversation, I am fine.

DIP YOUR TOE INTO THE WATER

Walking into an event is similar to getting into a hot bath. First you put your toe into the water, and then your foot and you gradually ease your way in. But at some point you've got to submerge yourself.

Start by talking to someone you know. It's fine to speak to existing contacts, particularly if you are looking to develop your relationship with them. The key is not to spend too long with the same people and then walk out complaining that 'that was a waste of time'.

> I remember an event that we held about three years ago in the head office of a major global corporate. There were about two hundred people present, a dozen of whom were representing the host company.
>
> The company had held the event to showcase their premises to potential customers, impress them with their generosity and provide their sales team with a captive audience to discuss how they could help them.
>
> Throughout the evening there were two groups of people in the room, about 190 small business owners networking with each other and the twelve hosts, huddled in a corner talking to each other, spending their time with the same people with whom they generally spent most of their working week.
>
> After the event we talked to the host company's representatives about networking. It became clear that the failure to mingle and the associated lost opportunity was a result of their fear of approaching people and the comfort of being in the company of their colleagues.

THE POWER OF INTRODUCTION

Once you have got the feel of the event and feel a bit bolder, you can then ask your associates to introduce you to someone they know. Have you noticed how if we're introduced to a stranger by a friend who knows him, we don't see him as a stranger and we don't have that same fear? So get a friend to introduce you to someone that he knows, or you introduce him to someone you know, and start talking.

The other advantage of this is that your companion, in introducing you, may well talk about how you have helped them, how great you are at what you do or praise you in another way that you would not have been able to do. This will awaken a greater interest in you from the new contact than may otherwise have been possible.

If there are specific people who you want to meet and you are nervous about approaching them, ask a colleague or the organiser if they know them. If they do, ask if they would be kind enough to introduce you. It will also help if you explain why you want to meet them; if they can understand your objectives, they will certainly be happier making the connection.

If you introduce someone else, make sure that you explain why you are making the connection and, if possible, the relevance your two contacts have for each other. Allow a conversation to start flowing before slipping away quietly.

If you and your companion both struggle to approach strangers and neither of you know anyone else in the room, take advantage of security in numbers to approach a group of people together. You will find that, after you have introduced each other, the group will naturally break up into smaller parties and you have smoothly moved into a conversation with a new person.

THE HOST WITH THE MOST

Act the host. If you see someone walking around on their own, go up and introduce yourself to them. Put your hand out and say "Hi, I'm Andy nice to meet you." (I would suggest you use your own name, but the principle remains the same!) Perhaps volunteer to act as a 'visitor host' if you are a member of a networking organisation. This will give you the opportunity to meet all of the new people coming into the room and you will feel more comfortable speaking to them, after all, that's your responsibility.

You don't need to be a volunteer to be a host, however. The renowned British business coach and networking trainer, George Metcalfe, often talks about the ability of children at their parent's parties to meet everyone there. Their mother or father gives them the crisps or nuts and invites them to pass around the room offering them to all of the guests.

I am not suggesting taking on the role of the waiters, but you can certainly start conversations by offering other people a top up of their drink or a selection from the buffet when you help yourself. In fact, the bar or buffet table is often one of the best places to start a conversation, as long as you don't permanently have a mouth full of food!

TALKING TO PLANTS

At networking events, I will often look to start a conversation with people who are on their own. It is much easier than breaking into a group conversation and the chances are they won't tell you to leave them alone and go away. Very few people go to networking events for solitude.

You can often find these people around the bar or buffet table (they've probably read the advice above!) or by the walls. Nervous people on their own seldom stand in the middle of a room unless they are milling around trying to pluck up the courage to approach someone. Often they will be admiring the art on the walls or the flora in the room, which gives you a nice topic with which to start a conversation.

When approaching these people you are already at an advantage because, they will both respect your courage (which they have probably lacked) and be grateful that you've taken the time and effort to relieve them from their anxiety. They are probably just as nervous as everyone else, and they'll be delighted to get into a conversation with you. You've rescued them from walking around, avoiding interrupting other people for fear of rejection.

When you do approach them, take care not to dive in aggressively but be empathetic to their nervous state. Ask them if they mind if you join them before introducing yourself, rather than running up asking, "So, what do you do then?"

Having spoken to them, try not to leave them on their own again because you'll just return them to the same state you found them. Move on with them and introduce them to someone else.

APPROACHING GROUPS

If you see a group of people talking, approach the group, but don't butt in. Remember, as Susan RoAne says in *How to Work a Room*, "There is a difference between *including* yourself in other people's conversations and *intruding* on them."

If someone's talking and you interrupt, or ask if you can join them, people will stop listening to the person who's talking, and invite you into their group. That's great for you but not so nice for the person who's talking. Stand just on the edge of the group and wait for the appropriate time.

The easiest way to approach a group is to catch the eye of one of the participants and smile. Usually they should invite you to join them at the appropriate juncture. Alternatively, it may be that they're talking about something in which you have an interest, in which case, when there's an appropriate pause, you can just say, "Excuse me, I heard you mention so and so. Can I ask you a question? Are you involved in that?" and you're in the conversation. Or it may just be that you have a pause, and you ask, "May I join you?" But it's always best to wait for the right pause in conversation.

The one thing I try to avoid is approaching two people who are in discussion. If you see two people talking together, they may be building a rapport and an interruption may break that. Alternatively, they may be discussing business.

At a networking event a couple of years ago at the New Zealand Embassy, I was talking to someone who was involved with an overseas Alumni Association. My colleague was informing me that the Association were looking for a place to meet in London. I spotted an opportunity for one of our clients to host the meetings in their corporate headquarters and possibly benefit from meeting some of the influential business people who I assumed were members.

I was just trying to find out enough information so I could make the connection when another guest approached us. I had met Annie at a number of other networking events and smiled as she approached but carried on with the conversation as I was in the middle of a question.

"Will representatives of my client's organisation be welcome to attend the meetings and would it be appropriate?" I asked.

"I am sure that wouldn't be a problem and they would probably be very welcome," came the reply.

Annie was standing alongside, with her head tilted and eyes intently focused on the two of us. From her mouth came sounds of agreement and interest, even though what we were talking about was so specific that it couldn't possibly have engaged her.

Not wanting to be rude, we felt obliged to break our conversation to invite her in. The conversation died and I left the two of them to talk. Fortunately, I followed the contact up myself, but not everyone will, and a very strong opportunity could have been lost.

While the guidelines above are important, you need to be aware of the body language of people talking to each other at networking events. Whether in couples or groups, people will send very clear signals about their approachability by the way they are standing.

If their body language is 'closed', and they are facing each other, you should avoid interrupting them. If they are more 'open' and they are standing at an angle that leaves room for another party in the conversation, you are likely to be more welcome.

Reading this body language may mean that you are better advised approaching two people rather than a group.

A MINUTE TO WIN IT

Many networking events invite attendees to stand up and present their business to other guests. Membership organisations such as the one for which I am Managing Director, Business Referral Exchange (BRE), invite members to give a sixty second presentation every week and, occasionally, a ten minute presentation. Some one–off events have similar 'introduce yourself' sessions; there are plenty of opportunities available.

And that's exactly what they are, opportunities. Our fear of speaking in public tells us otherwise and most people will be more inclined to run the other way or hide under the table. But that means passing up a valuable opportunity that may have led to business or other lucrative contacts.

I remember being invited to give a presentation at an event in Walsall, West Midlands, in January 2005. The organiser of the event held a business card draw for people to give a one minute pitch to everyone who was there. They were offering up to three opportunities to pitch, but there were only two cards in the hat, out of sixty people present!

One of the people who did take the opportunity worked for one of the major banks. There were three other bankers in the room that morning, but I only found that out afterwards. Everyone knew about at least one of the banks, the one who had the courage to put his name into the hat.

This is not the only time when I've found people reluctant to take advantage of an opportunity to promote their business. After all, if you are at any event representing your business, why wouldn't you take advantage of the opportunity to tell people about what you can offer?

On another occasion I was speaking in 2003 at an exhibition in Earls Court, London. It was a three–day exhibition and the day after my talk I returned to have a proper look round at the exhibition.

I was walking past the seminar room I had presented in the day before and heard a speaker called Mike Southon, well known for his 'Beermat' series of books.

Mike was asking for volunteers from the audience.

"Come on," Mike was saying, "Who's going to be next?"

There was no reply.

"This is a fantastic opportunity," Mike continued. "Do I have no more volunteers?"

Despite the room being packed, there was still no response. I looked at the programme schedule at the door and the event taking place was billed as 'A Minute to Win It'. Mike was offering his audience the opportunity to present their business to a packed room for sixty seconds, and no–one was taking him up on the opportunity.

Sitting in the audience was Joanna, a young business woman whom I had met the day before. I knew that she was intelligent, confident and quite capable of presenting her business. I asked her if she had taken the opportunity yet, she shook her head. I encouraged her to go for it, but she didn't feel ready, "Maybe next time," she said.

When would next time come around? The exhibition was on its last day. It would not be back for another year, and there was no guarantee that they would repeat the session or that she would be able to attend.

I volunteered to speak, went up to the stage and took the microphone from Mike. I was more nervous giving my sixty second presentation there than I had been speaking for forty–five minutes the day before, because I hadn't been able to prepare. But I still did it and I had seven enquiries about what I do as a result.

Joanna was afraid of looking foolish, the same fear of rejection that afflicts us when we walk into a room full of strangers. Once again, a fear without foundation.

When we attend a networking event and listen to speakers, we tend to listen to learn, not to judge. So when the opportunities to speak at such events come up, remind yourself that you know more about your business than your audience, that you have something to offer them. They want to accept your offer rather than mark you on your performance.

And what if it goes wrong? I have been present on more than one occasion when someone has stood up to give a presentation and lost their thread, dried up or simply panicked and sat down again. And it was fine, no one judged them, no one laughed or put their heads in the hands. Certainly no one judged their business based on their struggle with their presentation. They knew that they had to have guts just to try it in the first place.

APPROACHING CELEBRITIES

There will be times when you find yourself in the same room as a celebrity. It may be a sporting hero, a popular author or a favourite actor from TV or the cinema. Questions will probably start racing through your mind. Should you approach them? If you do, what can you say? How can you avoid looking like a fool?

Similarly you may find yourself at a networking event where you particularly admire the guest speaker and would like to meet her. Many people will not take the opportunity because of the same questions haunting their thoughts.

On one occasion I attended a meeting where the guest speaker was a very successful UK businessman. I wanted to meet him to ask if he would be interested in helping me with my next book. As soon as the formal part of the event had finished and people were mingling, I made my way over to his table.

Someone was already speaking to him, so I waited patiently. When he was free, I introduced myself and explained how I thought he could help with the book. He was visibly delighted as his eyes lit up. At that point, the momentum of the relationship changed, he clearly was interested in speaking to me.

Soon afterwards, I was with another delegate at the event when the businessman walked past. As he did, my colleague whispered, "please talk to me, please talk to me." I explained that he would, I

> was sure, be happy to. I didn't think he had travelled a long way to that event to be left alone.
>
> A while later, as I left at the end of the event, the speaker stopped me to make sure that I would be in touch. As he did, I noticed who he was speaking quite happily to – my colleague from earlier.

It is important to remember that most successful business people have built their success from scratch and they have needed the help of a lot of people along the way. As their businesses grow, the majority do not shut themselves away and, if they did, they wouldn't choose networking events to do so.

Many people will shy away from approaching a speaker at events because they feel that they are 'not worthy' of the person's attention. This is a misguided attitude; the speaker often feels out on a limb after their talk and welcomes people's approaches.

One suggestion though – not all speakers welcome 'constructive criticism' on their talks, particularly straight afterwards! By all means tell them how much you enjoyed it, but remember that speaking in public is the second major fear after walking into a room full of strangers. However successful they may have been in business, they are overcoming both fears in one session, and may well have been consumed with nerves as a result!

Remember to treat them with respect, but not to resort to fawning over them. As Leil Lowndes says in her book *How to Talk to Anyone*, "big shots don't slobber."

You can't succeed at networking by hiding on your own or by limiting your network by not speaking to anyone new. Just be courageous – it's nice when you meet new people, it's fantastic when people show an interest in what you do. That's what these events are all about.

So that's your first tip – be courageous.

TIP 2 – Be Committed

"When you get right down to the root of the meaning of the word succeed, you find that it simply means to follow through."
F.W. Nichol

So you're at a networking event, you've overcome your fears and started to talk to people and develop a few interesting conversations. What happens next is the key to making networking a success for you.

The easy approach is to enjoy a pleasant conversation with someone you meet, you say goodbye, move on and never see them again for the rest of your life. But what is that going to achieve? Networking is about building relationships, where you help others and they help you over time.

If you want networking to benefit you, you need to be committed to the process. That commitment starts before the event you are attending, extends to the time you are actually at the event and keeps going even after you have left.

DOES YOUR PHONE RING BY ITSELF?

It is vital that you work out how important networking is to your business. Caroline Heward, of Vitality Total Wellbeing, is renowned in London as an energetic and enthusiastic networker.

As President of the London Junior Chamber of Commerce and Chairman of the Bond Street BRE Group, many people comment about the amount of networking she does.

Caroline's response is, "People are my business; networking is my business. I need the referrals from people. If I stayed at home, the phone wouldn't ring."

DO YOU KNOW WHAT SUCCESS LOOKS LIKE?

Just going out and networking is not the most effective way to succeed. Before you join a group, attend an event or sign up for membership online, ask yourself some simple questions, such as:

- Why are you joining?
- What do you want to achieve from your participation?
- Is this event or organisation best suited to meet your needs?
- What do you need to do to make sure that those needs are met?
- What will success look like to you?

Many people will network because other people tell them that it will benefit them or their business, but they don't stop to work out what those benefits will be or what they will look like. Many high achievers will tell you, it is much harder to reach a target if you didn't know you were aiming for it in the first place.

Setting goals from networking may seem pointless when also given advice to build relationships and to give without expecting in return. It may not appear to sit comfortably with the suggestion that you should not look for a sale or for potential customers at an event.

The two approaches do go hand in hand. If the goals you set are longer term, the relationships you build and the events you attend can help you to achieve them. It is when people set short term goals that they tend to struggle.

GOAL SETTING FOR NETWORKING

As with any other business strategy, you need to know what the acceptable return on investment (ROI) would be from your networking. Would you embark upon any other marketing campaign without being able to measure its success?

Initially you need to work out what your networking costs you. Not just in subscriptions and meeting costs, but also in time and opportunity cost.

Ask yourself:

- What else could you have been doing instead of networking?
- How productive would that have been for your business?
- How important would that have been for your personal life?

These all need to be factored into the equation.

When you have a figure that represents the *minimum* return you are looking for from your networking activities, break that down to calculate the easiest and quickest way of achieving it.

A BRE Group was asked what they thought their minimum ROI might be from their membership of this organisation?

A mortgage broker, Maher George, responded with a figure of £30,000 in commission.

"Great," I said, "what does that look like?"

Maher was confused, perhaps imagining a line of suitcases crammed with money, so I asked the question in a different way.

"What is your average commission?"

"That depends, it could be £500, it could be £15,000," came the reply.

With a simple question like this, suddenly the figure of £30,000 becomes much more achievable. To reach this level of commission from his networking activities, Maher could aim to win two pieces of business worth £15,000 each to him or sixty mortgage deals worth £500. Or, more likely, a mixture in between.

With that in mind, Maher could plan his approach. Surely he needs to be connected to different people to win the high commission business compared to the low return mortgages? In the case of the £500 commission, Maher would probably be better advised to look for connections to estate agents or surveyors who could refer him rather than find a large number of people looking for new mortgages direct.

When looking for introductions to people requiring substantial lending, Maher could now paint a clear picture of who they are and how to recognise them, because he recognises himself that they are the people to whom he wants to speak.

INTANGIBLE REWARDS

As we have already discussed, not everybody networks purely for the financial return. Many people are looking for other benefits, from peer group support and a trusted network of suppliers to a reliable source of information and even social benefits.

During a recent visit to the Leeds Rothwell BRE Group one member there told me that she predominantly attended the meetings to improve her confidence. She had set up her own company six months previously and, prior to doing so, had only worked for large firms in a very safe and supportive environment and had never had to 'go it alone' before.

The discipline of attending a meeting of experienced business people every week and having to stand and present her business was giving her great focus and really building her confidence.

When looking at the ROI from networking activities, and setting goals to achieve that return, these 'intangible' benefits also need to be considered and factored into the equation. But how easily can they be measured?

You may need to be a bit more imaginative when setting goals to achieve these benefits, but it can be done. For example, the member who was looking to increase her self–confidence could aim to present a seminar on her business within a year. Someone looking for peer group support could aim to identify one issue within their business every month to discuss with their network.

The key is that you recognise what will contribute to success from your networking and focus on it. By doing so, you will also find it much easier to motivate yourself to attend events that you are dreading. Attending events with a sense of purpose will make a huge difference to your confidence when there.

PLANNING FOR THE MEETING

Attending a meeting once and telling yourself that it has been a waste of time because no direct business has resulted may be a missed opportunity. You need to look at the aims of the meeting, the contacts you have made and the long–term potential of the relationships that could be forged.

Before attending any event, find out what you should expect and what is expected of you.

- Will you be required to make a presentation?
- Will there be twenty people there or two hundred?
- Is the meeting designed as a sales opportunity for the attendees or as an information and knowledge exchange?

You should then look at how this fits into your networking business plan and set your expectations accordingly.

When there remember to 'be in the moment'. If you are purely focused on your goals and don't allow for the random connections that will help you to achieve them, they will not help you. You will come across to other people as very closed, rather than being open to them. This, as we are about to find out, would be a fatal error.

BE IN THE ROOM

Once at the event, you need to be committed to the other people there. This applies particularly to the person with whom you are speaking or to whose presentation you are listening. Some people spend their time looking over the shoulder of the person they are engaged in conversation with, planning who they are going to speak to next or working out where the nearest drinks waiter is.

I have spoken to people who have met leaders like Richard Branson, Tony Blair, Margaret Thatcher, George W. Bush and even Winston Churchill. They have all told me how they felt as if there was no–one else in the room when they were speaking to them. However short the conversation, they felt as if they were the centre of the universe throughout. You need to ensure that when you are speaking to someone, you are in the room for them the whole time.

Similarly, if somebody is giving a presentation, pay them the courtesy of listening. By listening, I mean listen *for* them, rather than to them.

Ask yourself:

- Why they are saying what they are?
- What can I do to help them?
- What could they do to help someone else I know?
- How might someone else in my network help them?

Again, be committed by being in the room for them.

When you are in conversation with somebody, make sure that you are making strong, positive eye contact with them. Your reactions should reflect your interest and reflect the points they are making. Smile at appropriate moments and be conscious all the time of what your body language is saying about you.

DEVELOPING RAPPORT

Practitioners of Neuro–Linguistic Programming (NLP) place a strong emphasis on the importance of reflecting body language in building rapport with another individual. The process of 'mirroring' what the other person is doing, how they are standing or the gestures they make makes them feel more at ease with you and it is increasingly likely that you will be able to develop a relationship with them.

However, while it is good to be aware of opportunities to mirror the other person, it is important that you remain natural. In one meeting with an NLP trainer, I asked if he minded if I moved from his couch, which I found uncomfortable and sat on the floor. He in turn asked if he could do the same.

His intention was to mirror my position and make me feel at ease, or 'in rapport', by speaking with me from the same level. However, his actions succeeded only in making me feel less comfortable because of his unnatural behaviour.

At another event I was discussing NLP techniques with someone when we noticed that we were in perfect rapport without really trying. It felt natural and we were getting on famously and we were both fully engrossed in our conversation.

Very often you will see people in natural rapport, mirroring each other, despite the fact that neither of them has probably come across NLP. Watch two friends in a pub discussing football (particularly if they support the same team!) or two lovers opposite each other at a table in a restaurant.

In *Networking for Success*, an excellent text on the role of NLP in networking, Carol Harris defines rapport as "the state which exists between people when they feel comfortable together and are 'on the same wavelength'."

So be in the room for others by focusing on them and showing a natural interest in what they are saying. Don't worry about who you want to speak to next or what you want to say, focus on *them* and you will find it much easier to develop the necessary rapport.

DO WHAT YOU SAY YOU ARE GOING TO DO

The commitment continues after the meeting. If you agree to do something, then do it. If you agree to follow someone up, then do so. The alternative is to build a reputation as someone who is not reliable. The real networking successes come from building relationships over a period of time. Carole Stone, a networking columnist for City AM in London, said, "Make friends when you can. You can't just do it when you need help."

If you meet someone at a networking event, and ten months down the line you think "that's the person I want to talk to" and you phone him, what are the chances of him remembering you?

Be committed to the process, do what you say you are going to do, and follow it up. Make sure that you do so promptly. The longer you leave your follow–up, the less chance there is that people will remember you and what you discussed.

Even if you have not agreed an action between you, or you have agreed to do something together in a few months' time, follow up immediately. Where an action has been agreed reiterate it in the follow–up or, if appropriate, do it. If you have promised to connect them with someone in your network, do so as soon as possible. When the connection is made their response will be stronger because your promise is fresh in their mind.

I find that the most effective immediate method of follow up is email. While letters and cards have much more impact in these electronic days, emails are quick, simple and tend to be kept for longer.

Email follow–ups should not be unnecessarily long and, unless your new contact has specifically asked for information about your company, should not contain any sales information. You can, however, include your website address or a brief sales message, as part of the signature at the foot of the email without causing offence.

I tend to email confirming that it was a pleasure to meet and reiterating any agreed actions. Try to make sure that the subject field of the email is clear and unlikely to find its way into the other person's spam folder. I often include the name or date of the event in the subject field to personalise it.

Once you have followed up initially you still face a strong chance of losing touch if you do not follow up on a regular basis. This is easy if you both attend the same event on a regular basis and those events can be used to build the relationship.

Time allowing, arrange meetings with the people with whom you have either developed the most rapport or where there may be a clear business synergy. I don't tend to have an agenda when I go into these meetings, it is important to me to allow our personalities to engage. If they do, other benefits tend to follow.

Maintain the relationship with your contacts by sending information that may be of interest to them, dropping them the odd line asking how they are, or best of all, connecting them to other people in your network. This is one of the hidden benefits of referring your contacts to each other; it helps you to keep in touch.

We will examine follow–up in greater detail later in the book.

When you attend a lot of networking events, it can be very difficult to keep in touch with everyone you meet and to build meaningful relationships with all of them. For a start, you will probably not find rapport with everyone and relationships cannot be forced.

If I attend a meeting with over one hundred people present, I would expect to speak to about twelve of them over the course of a couple of hours. If I go away with between five and seven business cards I am happy and if I develop one or two long–term relationships as a result the event has been a success.

BE SELECTIVE WITH YOUR CARD

I don't give my card out to everyone I meet. I give my card out either if I am asked for it, or if I want the other person to have it for a reason. I'm not in business to fund printers nor to fund the recycling industry. What happens to business cards that you collect at networking events when you get back to your office? If people haven't made an impression on you or if you can't remember what they do, where do you 'file' their card?

I walked into a networking event in Scotland recently to be greeted by one of the members. Before I had even introduced myself, he had given me two of his business cards.

Later in the same meeting, one of the visitors to the group asked for the member's card. He was passed two, and everyone in the room was invited to take two cards if he did not already have them.

How would you feel if someone gave you two of his cards? It's a bit presumptuous, don't you think?

I was speaking to someone towards the end of a networking event in Croydon in 2001. Someone I know came up to me to say goodbye. He turned to the lady to whom I was speaking to apologise for interrupting and asked if they had met that evening.

"No, we haven't," came the reply.

"Here's my card then," he responded, passing across one from a large pile of business cards.

I asked him a year or so later if had ever heard from the lady I had been speaking to. "Of course not," he replied, "and I am more selective in how I use my cards now."

At many networking meetings where people are seated for formal business, people are encouraged to pass their business cards around the room. Some groups even have a card box for this purpose.

There are two key problems with this. The first is the lack of recognition. While people may take your card if they are interested in your service, with a lack of a connection between the two of you, their interest will soon wane. If they have taken your card, along with everyone else's, by the time they get back to their office they are likely to discard it if they cannot remember you or see an immediate use for your services.

Secondly, if the cards are being passed around during formal business there are likely to be at least three people not participating or listening; the person looking through the cards; the person going through the cards they have just collected; the person waiting to receive the cards next.

This problem becomes greater if different bundles of cards are being circulated individually, as more people are probably looking through business cards than are listening to the presentations being made.

MAKE THE CONNECTION

The CEO of a networking organisation in the United States took on someone to run their groups in Georgia. They picked this person because of her reputation as a great networker. The CEO accompanied his new partner to a business meeting and watched as she ran around the room talking to people and collecting their business cards.

At the end of the event she had a pile of business cards that surely represented most people in the room. They went back to her office where she entered all of the details onto her contact management system, already crammed with hundreds of names and numbers.

Six months later, she had failed to get a single group off the ground. She had contacted everyone on her database, people whose business cards she had collected when she had met them at events.

The key was that she had met people at events and taken their card without making a connection. As a result, the response to her many emails was as low as an average cold–calling campaign – because nobody knew who she was.

I won't refer someone to a contact who may need their services just because I have their business card. I will refer them because they have made an impression on me and they are in my mind at the right time. I can't carry around the business cards of everyone I meet at networking events, but I can carry around my memory.

For a referral to be effective, I will be more likely to pass on the details of the potential contact rather than simply handing out one of the supplier's cards.

WRITE THINGS DOWN

I only ask for someone's business card if I am going to use it to prompt me to do something to follow up our conversation. I used to think it would be rude if I wrote on someone's business card in front of them, so I'd sit on the train after networking events, or at my desk the next day if I had been driving, going through the cards I had collected, trying to work out who was who and what we had agreed.

Now, if I say I'm going to do something, I will write on the back of that person's card there and then. The next day, or sometimes it's two or three days later when I get into the office, I can remember who they are, I can remember what our conversation was, and I can follow it up.

If you are going to do this be aware of cultural differences. My habit of writing on the back of a business card in front of its owner may be perfectly acceptable in Western environments but it is frowned upon in Asia. Business cards are held in much higher esteem there, and there is a ritual in how you hand over cards, how you receive them and how you study them. You should certainly never, ever write on them.

THE WHY, WHAT AND HOW

From your planning, through the meeting, to the follow–up you need to have a strong focus on why you are there, what you want to achieve and how you can help others. You need to be in the room for other people as well as for yourself and must ensure that you don't waste the effort by throwing away the contacts made.

Remember that the need to be committed to networking is the same as the need to use the facilities regularly when you join a health club. You can pay your subscription to the gym but if you don't attend and work out effectively, you will still be just as unfit!

If you are going to network effectively, the second tip is "be committed". So be courageous and be committed.

TIP 3 – Be Patient

"All good things arrive unto them that wait."
Mark Twain

This is a commonly held belief and one very relevant to networking. We have already established that networking success comes from building relationships over a period of time. Consistent networking results can only come as people develop trust in you and an understanding of how they can help you.

If you are looking for people to refer you, they need to be able to recognise opportunities for you and think of you when those opportunities arise. That doesn't tend to happen too often with people we have only briefly met.

Andrew Ferdinando is the former National Business Development Manager for Regus Serviced Offices in the UK. In his earlier days in Regus they used to sponsor an evening networking event in the City of London. Each time that Andrew went to an event he was charged by his employers to come back with five leads, with the expectation that at least two would convert into business.

"I am so embarrassed when I look back at it now," Andrew said to me during a recent meeting. "At the end of every event the organiser would ask me what I thought about it and I would tell him how disappointed we were and how we didn't feel that we were getting value for our sponsorship. It is so easy to see in retrospect how wrong we were, and when we came back to networking a couple of years later, we came with a completely different attitude. But I feel so bad about how we treated that organiser. We simply didn't understand networking."

'QUALITY PEOPLE'

I am often told by people that they want to attend events where they will meet 'quality people'. I must admit that I have a problem knowing which events to recommend.

I'm never sure what people mean when they talk about 'quality people'. I assume that they are not talking about the education, manners, altruism or intelligence of the people attending the event. More often than not, they are looking to meet senior executives or decision makers in large companies.

I have two questions to ask people who look to attend events where these decision makers are present. The first one is, if invitation depends on status, and you are not on a par with these 'quality people', how do you get to go to the event that they will attend?

The second question is, if 'quality people' were to attend these events, how would you approach them and what would you discuss with them? My feeling is that the discourse would be one way, as you are 'targeting' these decision makers. The outcome would neither benefit you in the long–term, nor would it encourage them to attend such events.

Many people will look at an attendee list and head straight for the person from a well–known national company, particularly one that they have targeted as a prospective client.

Such people, however, are likely to be more focused on sales within the company rather than charged with making buying decisions. In a large organisation they can be further removed from the decision makers within their organisation than many other attendees at the event.

There are events at which you can meet prospective customers from big companies, and these are 'meet the buyer' events, where everyone has a specific purpose for being there and it is OK to sell.

You can meet senior decision makers at big companies through networking events, but perhaps the 'quality people' you wanted to meet are not who you thought they were.

AVOID PRECONCEPTIONS

When we go along to networking events most of us look at who is present and ask ourselves who we need to speak to, who our potential customers are and who we consider to be a waste of time.

This approach can severely hamper our prospects as we may write off people who can prove to be the perfect introducers for us or spend too long trying to sell to someone who may never want to buy.

I'm not a great fan of statistics and I believe that a common figure often repeated in books and conversations about networking is extremely conservative. Top US salesman, Joe Girard's, 'Law of 250' states that every person, on average, knows at least 250 other people. This would seem to me extremely low. I would venture that the number in my personal network currently extends into four figures and I don't think I am unusual in that respect.

Think of all of the people who you know or who you could easily reconnect with. They may be clients, suppliers, friends, family, networking contacts or business associates. Perhaps they include people who you have met at the golf club, at Rotary events, on the school run or at a friend's dinner party. I would also include former work colleagues, neighbours or school and university friends. You just have to witness the success of Friends Reunited to realise the power of the latter network.

Now ask yourself:

- What does each of those people do for a living?
- What does their husband or wife do?
- Who do they meet through their work every day?
- Who are their friends and what do they do?

The people who you meet at networking events will share a similar network. They have the ability to connect you to many types of people, from housewives and school teachers, through engineers and nuclear scientists to the Chief Executive Officers of global corporations.

When you first meet someone you can have no way of knowing how they may be able to help you, or to whom they may be able to connect you. You will not know when they may be the key contact you need or what they could do for you in future.

It may be that there is no clear connection between the two of you, yet they could be the ideal person to refer to someone else in your network or you may know the perfect person to help them.

A name badge or a business card is not going to tell you this. It takes time to speak to people, to ask them questions and get to know them before it becomes clear how they fit into your network.

THE SIX DEGREES OF SEPARATION

In 1967 Professor Stanley Milgram developed a theory so widely recognised now that books have been written, television programmes made and even a film produced based around the idea. That theory is one of *Six Degrees of Separation* and states that we are only six steps away from anyone in the world. I have seen the theory proved time and time again.

In his experiment, Professor Milgram mailed a name and address to 160 people who lived in Omaha, Nebraska. In every package the name was the same, a stockbroker who lived in Sharon, Massachusetts and who worked in Boston. Each recipient was asked to write their own name on the package and post it onto someone who they knew on a first name basis and who they thought most likely to know the broker. That person would then write their own name on the package and send it on a step closer in turn.

Once all of the packages had been received by the broker, Milgram was able to track back through the steps each package had taken on its journey. He found that most of the packages had taken five or six steps to reach its destination.

I received an email in 2003 from one of our members, saying, "I want to test the theory of Six Degrees of Separation. Who do you know who can introduce me to President Putin of Russia?"

Angela Sherman, who wrote this email, is a copywriter, and one of her clients, Richard Meredith, is a travel writer who was travelling around the world at the time. Driving from Luton to South Korea, he had reached Azerbaijan and was weighing up his options. Angela takes up the story from here:

"Richard's route had so far taken him across Western Europe and on into central Asia. His original plan had been to head into China from Kyrgyzstan and then to drive all the way across to Shanghai before taking a boat to South Korea. However, entry restrictions and tedious obstructions with paperwork and documentation meant that this now seemed impossible. So Plan B came into force: Russia!

There's nothing like laying down a challenge. To me it simply had to be taken up. And so I sent an email to my colleagues at my regular BRE Group in Wavendon, Milton Keynes, and to our BRE Head Office contacts, Andy and Michael. I simply asked if they knew someone who knew someone who might know someone who ... knew President Putin – or the Chinese leader.

I suspected they'd all think I was nuts. I suspect you might too! Well, the good news is I'm not nuts. Huge relief! Here's what happened ...

Michael rang me to tell me that he plays golf with the father of the BBC's senior correspondent in Russia. Fantastic news! (Pardon the pun.)

A member of my own group had a Commercial Attaché contact within a Russian Embassy in a key strategic location en route. How good is that!

Andy put me in touch with a contact, who is ex–Foreign Office Chinese Affairs and now works to help people build relationships with China and get through the bureaucracy. He has direct links with the Chinese government. Pretty impressive!

Another member of my group is a Labour Party member and has a close link with Tony Blair. This may seem tenuous but with the warming relationship between Blair and Putin, plus the Party link, that's a very viable contact in this respect.

Andy offered to put me in touch with a former MP with excellent international contacts. This just gets better!

And Andy also put me in touch with a visitor to Blackpool BRE who could help my client cross out of Azerbaijan, together with a new BRE Member whose wife's father used to be the Chinese Ambassador to Canada. Phenomenal!

I was bowled over by the response. These contacts mean I'm just one, perhaps two, steps away from both the Russian and the Chinese leaders! Remarkable."

For most of us, while it is nice to know that we are so close to the corridors of power, it is more important to know that we can connect to people much closer to home. Many people will be looking for connections to people in business in the same country as us and the good news is that we are unlikely to need the full six degrees to make the contact.

How often have you met people with connections to your old school, your workplace or other people in your network and laughed with them at how small the world is? Each time it happens we tend to be amazed at the coincidence but perhaps we really do live in a 'small world' – a world that is made even smaller by modern communications.

You are no more than six steps away from anyone in the world. If you are aware of this, the potential of networking becomes so much greater. This is particularly true if you are looking to speak to someone who is also in business and is in the same region, or even country, as you. In these cases, you will probably be much closer than you think.

At one BRE meeting near Birmingham recently, one member asked for connections to Sir Richard Branson, the founder of the Virgin Group. Of the seventy–three people present, three had connections and none of them was more than three steps away.

In June 2005 I was speaking at the GiS Sales Club in Birmingham. A few weeks before the event six thousand workers at the nearby Rover car plant had been made redundant.

As a result of something I had said in my talk, David Hyner, one of the organisers of the Club, told the delegates that he wanted to put on a day of seminars for redundant workers who wanted to set up their own businesses.

David stood at the front of the room and asked who people knew who could introduce them to redundant workers or who could help move the project forward. As he was asking this, Stewart Evans, a BRE Regional Partner for the Midlands, walked to the front and started to write on a flipchart.

Now, given the amount of breakfast meetings he has to attend, Stewart is not the smallest of people. As David tried to carry on, everyone else was craning their necks, trying to see around Stewart to see what he was writing. We had to wait until he stepped away, revealing the words...

"I know the HR Director of Rover."

Sometimes it really is that simple!

Of course, the more links there are in the chain before you get to your ideal connection, the more diluted your message will be and the weaker the relationship is with your contact, making it harder to make an effective connection. That is not to say that it cannot still be done, but you need to focus on making your message very strong. We will look at this later in the book.

YOU DON'T KNOW WHO THEY KNOW

When you go into a networking event, don't look at the person you meet and think, "what are you going to do for me? Are you going to buy from me?" Don't make any prejudgement about their relevance to your life. You don't know who they know. Pursue the relationship, get to know them, and then ask for what you want at the appropriate time and you may find it will come to you.

The key is to build the relationships to a level where, when people have the connections you may be seeking, they are comfortable with introducing you. That takes time, so you must be patient.

So those are your three tips for networking successfully:

1. Be courageous.
2. Be committed.
3. And then be patient, and the results will come your way.

THREE TOOLS

TOOL 1 – Pursue The Relationship, Not The Sale

"If you make listening and observation your occupation you will gain much more than you can by talk."
Robert Baden–Powell

One of the best compliments I received was unintended. While on a trip to Asia, my travelling companion and I joined a group of British business people who were on a training course.

I was introduced as a speaker on networking and someone who ran networking events back in the UK. During the evening the organiser turned around to my companion and asked a simple question, "Why isn't he networking? Surely this is a fantastic opportunity for him."

What he hadn't realised was that I had been networking. In fact, I had been networking very effectively. I had spoken with a number of the delegates that evening and I had been given a number of business cards from people who asked me to get back in touch when I returned to England and to arrange meetings to discuss business.

The key was that I hadn't been running around the room trying to make sure that I spoke to everyone there. Instead I had allowed conversations to flow naturally and discussed business when others were interested and asked me. In short, nobody felt 'networked' and I enjoyed the evening by being myself.

The best networkers do not visibly 'network'.

FINDING THE FLOW

Picture yourself at a networking event talking to somebody for the first time. You have asked them what they do and they are telling you, in detail, about their business. It is not a business that you have an interest in or something you have a need for.

You then tell them about your business and the same applies. They have the same blank look and vacant smile on their face as they politely listen to what you have to say, as you did before. When you have finished explaining what you do, you both smile, look uncomfortably around the room before making your excuses, shaking hands and moving on.

This is not an uncommon scene at such events. General networking events randomly put people together who do not have an interest in each others' field of expertise and then we expect conversation to flow. When we go to a networking event we talk about business because that is why we are there. But networking can be so much more productive if you focus on meeting the person before you worry about meeting the business.

IT'S OK TO TALK ABOUT FOOTBALL!

Think of the business people with whom you have a strong relationship. If there wasn't a strong shared business interest originally, how did the relationship develop? What was it that brought you together in the first place?

It is likely that the relationship has developed through something in common other than business, whether it is a hobby, your age and background, your lifestyle or other common experiences.

> I went along to one of our training events near Manchester in 2003. There were twelve people there, most of whom had not met each other prior to the event. Before breakfast people networked and the conversation was generally the same, everyone explaining who they were and what they did.
>
> As we sat down to breakfast, the table went silent. No–one there knew what to say next, after all, they had exhausted the limited business conversation they could have at that stage. The organiser of the training day mentioned to the person seated next to him that I had travelled up the day before and had been to see the Blackburn v. Charlton football match the previous evening. On finding out that I am a Charlton fan, the member mentioned that

he supported Everton and we started to discuss the success (or otherwise) of our respective clubs that season.

Other people with an interest in football soon joined in and in a short time there was plenty of discussion around the breakfast table, and not just about football. We had basically said that it was OK not to discuss business despite attending a business event.

As people find they have interests in common, so relationships begin to form.

It is the growth of a strong relationship that leads to successful networking. That doesn't arise from forced conversation about business; more from a relaxed conversation about common areas of interest.

If people ask about my business when we first meet at a networking event, I know that it is because that is what is expected, that they are being courteous. Asking someone 'what do you do' as a conversation opener in a networking event is the business equivalent of the 'do you come here often' chat–up line. That hasn't worked too often for me either!

I would always prefer someone to ask me about my business because they are genuinely interested rather than out of courtesy. That is only likely to happen when I have built a strong relationship with them.

CONVERSATION STARTERS

There are many natural ways to open a conversation without asking what the other person's business is. Much depends on the nature of the event and the environment you are in. With a little bit of imagination you can quickly get your partner talking about themselves and make sure that you find them interesting.

As Leil Lowndes says, "Big Cats never ask outright "What do you do?" (Oh, they find out alright, in a much more subtle manner.) Their silence says 'a man or woman is far more than his or her job'."

I find that you can trigger an interesting conversation where you both have something in common by talking about the event that you are at or the organisation behind it. Find out if your partner is a member of the organisation or if it is their first visit. What they are hoping to get out of it or what benefits have they seen in the past? Have they tried other types of networking locally or further afield?

This type of conversation opener can naturally lead to discussing each other's business, but in this case it is as a result of natural progression rather than forced and feigned interest. You can also find out more quickly how you can help your partner and they will be more likely to listen for you when discussing the results you are looking for from your attendance or membership.

If someone has an interesting business card or business name, ask about it. How did they come up with the name? Find out if there is a story behind it. Immediately you are on very strong ground, encouraging your partner to talk about a story that will probably mean a lot to them and helping you to find out more about them, their company and what makes them tick.

FLYING HIGH

Very often, when you find yourself talking about mutual passions, business can spring unexpectedly from the conversation.

> Anthony Smith–Roberts is a Health and Safety Consultant in the Milton Keynes Central BRE Group. Anthony has a passion for aircraft and was discussing that passion with the accountant in his BRE Group, who shares his interest.
>
> A friend of the accountant was also interested in aircraft and was involved with Coventry Airport. As a result of that conversation, Anthony was referred to the airport and now has the contract to cover about 80% of the health and safety there.
>
> Not only was this a fairly substantial piece of business but it opened the door for Anthony to tender for further health and safety contracts at UK airports from a position of experience.

NETWORKING IS ABOUT PEOPLE

Networking is not about selling; networking is about people. How many people go to networking predominantly to buy from others? And how many people go to networking events predominantly to sell their business, or to increase their business? I would venture to suggest that most will fall into the latter category. If that is the case, surely it is foolish to go to an event to sell to people who are not in buying mode.

I go to events to learn – and to enjoy myself. As I said at the beginning of this book, I have learnt so much since I became involved in networking and the bonus is that I have had a tremendous time doing it.

A wordsmith by the name of Peter Baxter–Derrington spoke at a BRE Group around the turn of the Millennium in Croydon. It was a time where we weren't sure if we were going into recession or not and Peter gave a talk about beating the recession. In talking about the need to network he said one thing that's stuck in my mind ever since. He said, "Pursue the relationship, not the sale."

"Pursue the relationship, not the sale." That's what networking is all about.

LISTENING *FOR* PEOPLE

Part of pursuing the *relationship*, not the *sale* is looking to help others rather than yourself. It's important that you are open to recognising those opportunities. It's also about following people up and being committed to the process.

Earlier in the book I mentioned that we should be listening *for* people to whom we are speaking. I think we get the English wrong. In the English language, we say we listen *to* people. That's *passive* – we should listen *for* each other. That implies something more proactive and that you are listening for a reason.

If you are at a networking event and someone is speaking to you about their business or about their personal life, they may be relating that personal information because they have a need to do that. Listen for them, and ask yourself in your mind "who do I know that this is relevant to? Who do I know that they could help? Who do I know who could help them?"

Stephen Covey, in his book *The Seven Habits of Highly Effective People*, discusses how we naturally listen to people while thinking about what we want to say next. We pick up the key words or phrases to convert into a story of our experiences or our thoughts. Or, as he puts it, people "listen with the intent to reply. They're either speaking or preparing to speak."

Covey encourages us to practise what he calls 'empathetic listening' or 'listening with intent to understand'. By endeavouring to understand where the other person is coming from, we are in a much stronger position to help them or to connect with them.

A little while ago I arranged to meet my co–author, Peter Roper, in Manchester as we were both working in the area. We wanted to talk about an idea for a seminar we had called '...and death came third!' I drove up to meet Peter, and we went to a place called Edward's Bar on a Wednesday evening at six o'clock.

A few people had clearly been celebrating very merrily so we perched at the end of the bar and waited until a table became available so that we could talk more privately.

Just after we found a table, a couple came over with a bottle of wine and asked if they could join us. It turned out that they had been on a table with a group who had been drinking since five o'clock, and they weren't quite drunk enough to enjoy the company. They obviously thought that we looked like better company. You can make mistakes on first impressions!

So they came and joined us, and Peter and I carried on our conversation, and they carried on with theirs. Gradually we began to chat to them. They were both in their mid–to–late twenties, both working in recruitment, and they were both looking for jobs in the Manchester area. Why is it that people in recruitment often struggle to find new jobs for themselves?

In the course of our conversation it turned out that one of the couple, Natasha, was very keen to find a job in advertising.

I mentioned that my brother–in–law is a Director of a large advertising agency in London.

When I mentioned the name of the company, Natasha was quite excited.

"Oh wow! That's the sort of company I want to get into!"

I said "I can't just ask Howard if he'll recruit you, but what I can do is ask him if he'll talk to you and give you some advice to help you to find the right position."

"Would he really do that?"

"Yes, I'm sure he will. All I want you to do is email me your details so I know you're serious." She did, and I put her in touch with my brother–in–law.

Then I said to Natasha, "If you're looking for work here, I'll put you in touch with Ed Nash, he's our Regional Partner in the North–West, and Ed knows everyone, he used to be in recruitment. He's one of the top networkers in the North–West of England. Have a chat with Ed, and go along to our breakfast meeting at Manchester Airport and meet some businesses there."

"Can I really? Can I really?"

"Of course you can!

"And ask Ed to introduce you to Will Kintish. Will is another speaker on networking and he predominately is based around the Manchester area, and he speaks to professional organisations – solicitors and accountants, so he knows a lot of people."

"Really? Are you sure? Why would you do all of this for me?"

"Because I can. Why not? What's it costing me to do this? You send me that email."

I was back to the office a few days later, and received the email I had asked for.

"Hi, do you remember me? We met in Edward's Bar, it's Natasha. You said you'd do this, here are my details."

So I made two phone calls. I phoned Ed and I phoned Howard, and I asked them if they would speak to Natasha if she phoned. They both replied, "Of course, no problem." I phoned Natasha and told her to phone them, passing on their details. That's all I did.

The next Tuesday I got a phone call from Natasha; "I don't know how to thank you! I'm speaking to your brother–in–law this afternoon, but I went to Manchester Airport this morning to your breakfast meeting and three people have phoned me between now and then! I left there three hours ago and one of them told me a client of theirs was looking for someone in marketing and would I be interested? And somebody else told me they knew someone who might be able to help me, and said they'd put me in touch!"

I spoke to Natasha again a couple of weeks later. I had been away on a stag weekend and, when talking to the groom's brother, found out that his girlfriend had a new job, for one of the biggest advertising agencies in London.

"Oh really, would she have a chat with Natasha about how she did it, because she was in a similar situation?"

"Oh she'll probably pass her CV on for her."

So I phoned Natasha to tell her and put her in touch.

A small ripple can create huge waves. It didn't take much to ask these people if they would speak to Natasha and the potential benefits for her were great. Don't ask yourself, "What's in it for me?" If it's easy and straightforward, just do it. If it costs you nothing to do, and it could get great results for the other person, just do it. Don't expect anything in return from that person.

If I had been listening *to* Natasha and not *for* her in that bar in Manchester, I wouldn't have recognised the opportunities for her. I probably wouldn't have developed a friendship and if I ever needed her help she wouldn't remember meeting me that evening in Edward's.

TRUST

Trust naturally plays a key role in networking, certainly when it comes to referring people. Many people would read the story above and question whether they would be happy to put a complete stranger in touch with valued contacts.

When I used to cold call companies to invite them along to BRE meetings, I often had to overcome the objection of "How can I refer to people who I don't know?" My response was very simple but very effective.

"Are there people to whom you refer now?"

"Yes, of course."

"Was there a time when you didn't know them?"

Of course, the answer to my second question could only be 'yes'. Trust has to be built up over a period of time. That's not to say that we cannot help, connect or do business with people with whom we haven't been able to build that trust.

I did not *trust* Natasha when I met her. That's not to say that I distrusted her, I just had not known her for long enough to build up a strong degree of trust. However, I was still happy to help her – why?

To build up trust, there needs to be a suspension of distrust first. You need to be prepared to place a small amount of faith in people in order to find out if they are worthy of a greater amount of your trust. That may be by using their services first, investing your time in getting to know them better or possibly by giving them *qualified referrals*.

In Natasha's case, I effectively gave her qualified referrals. When I told my brother–in–law and Ed Nash about Natasha, I told them that I had just met her a couple of days earlier. From that statement, they knew that I wasn't vouching for her abilities or reliability, I merely felt comfortable opening a couple of doors for her.

As people build relationships, so trust develops and referrals that were once qualified become strong, positive connections. Contracts that were perhaps initially small and unimportant become major.

So *pursue the relationship, not the sale*. That's tool number one.

TOOL 2 – People Are Interested In People Who Are Interested In Them

"I keep six honest serving–men, (They taught me all I knew);
Their names are What and Why and When
And How and Where and Who."
Rudyard Kipling

Remember the situation I outlined at the beginning of the last chapter? You are in a conversation with someone in whose business you don't have a real interest, but you want to develop the conversation to find out if you can establish the rapport that will lead to the relationship.

Dale Carnegie said, "People are interested in people who are interested in them" so, show an interest. If what they are saying does not interest you, lead them into other areas that may do. Ask questions about their business; questions to find their area of speciality; questions to discover their passion – eventually you'll find an area of common interest or something that they do that is of interest to you.

Jeffrey Mayer, in his book *Creating Opportunities by Networking* says, "When you talk about yourself, you're a bore. When you let the other person talk about himself, you're a great conversationalist."

SEND YOUR ELEVATOR PITCH TO THE BASEMENT!

In picking up this book on networking and presentation skills you probably expected some advice and guidance on writing and presenting the perfect 'elevator pitch'. This is the ten, thirty or sixty second script that you repeat word for word when someone asks what you do. This is your chance to grab your moment in the spotlight and shine!

If you have been looking for this, I am sorry to disappoint you. You may already have gathered that I would not be a fan of such a pre–prepared presentation in a networking environment. 'Elevator pitches' (so named because they represent what you would say if you met Bill Gates in an elevator and had until his floor to get him to want to hear more) may be fine when you have a 'Minute to Win It' slot to present to everyone at an event, but they can be out of place in a one–to–one situation or in a small group.

Yes, you should know what you do and why you are there, but do you really need to memorise a script in order to answer those questions? You will be far more relaxed and natural if you just tell people. Instead of being tense and stilted, people will experience the real you, a relaxed conversationalist.

ASKING THE RIGHT QUESTIONS

The key to good conversation is listening effectively and if you are listening effectively, you ask the right questions. That doesn't mean you ask the questions that you've seen listed in a book.

"So, are you married?"

"What colour is your dog?"

"Do your children like sports?"

These make you sound like a person who has read a book with a list of questions to ask at networking events! It doesn't make you sound interesting to the other person or interested in them. People can generally tell when you are genuinely engaged in the conversation, so you need to develop that interest.

Ask questions that show that you are listening, questions based on what the other person has just said and questions that are likely to draw out the conversation. Ask them to tell you more.

One key is to ask 'open questions', such as 'how?', 'why?', 'what?' and 'where?' that encourage your partner to open up and tell you more and give them permission to go into more detail. You should certainly avoid 'closed questions' that require a 'yes' or 'no' response and this will leave you faced with a dead end and struggling to move the conversation further on.

As you ask these questions you will find yourself becoming more drawn into the conversation and the questions will come more and more naturally. When people start talking about their passion they tend to become more animated and, generally, more interesting. You will find yourself learning more and being in a better position to connect the people you meet.

Listening isn't about tilting your head and staying silent. Listening is about being curious. If you really want to sell, a salesman will call that research, find out more about the other person and their needs.

From a networking point of view, however, it's simply getting into a conversation where the other person is interested.

I have been *speed networking*, where you are asked to listen to someone else talking about their business for three minutes without interrupting and then swap roles. A key benefit of speed networking events is that they enable you to meet a number of people in a short time, therefore, giving you a greater chance of increasing your network and supposedly making key connections. However, I struggle; I find that I can't just listen for that period of time. I feel totally disengaged. If the other person does say something of interest to me, I want to ask questions. I rarely spend my three minutes talking about my business because I still want to find out about the other person's.

Interestingly, I have found that the people who I have met whilst speed networking have been less likely to respond to my follow–up contacts, even if I have been offering to put them in touch with someone who may be interested in their services. I can only reason that this is because there was little opportunity to make a real connection and develop rapport in a forced conversation against a strict time limit.

CONTROLLING THE SITUATION

When you are asking questions and encouraging the other person to tell you more you will find yourself controlling the conversation. That, in turn, will help you to feel more confident. If you establish that confidence and control it also ensures that you come across as a reliable and interesting person, which makes it more likely that you will make a strong, positive impact. It is likely that the person to whom you are speaking will want to know more about you.

This doesn't mean that you should conduct the conversation like an interview, make sure that you are fully engaged rather than simply trying to direct. The questioning style you use should portray genuine interest.

WOULD YOU LIKE SOME ADVICE?

As people are telling you more about their business and the situations that they are looking to resolve through networking, you may find yourself in a position where you feel able to offer them advice. This might be by telling them how you dealt with a similar situation.

Be very careful about how you deal with situations like this. You destroy all of your hard work by immediately making the conversation revolve around you rather than your companion. Feel free to make suggestions, or ask if they have considered a different approach but it is often better to stop short of telling people how they should deal with a situation. Certainly ask their permission first before telling them about your experiences. And bring the conversation back to their problem as quickly as possible.

CONNECTIVITY = ATTRACTIVENESS

When you are listening, ask yourself how you can help the other person and how you might be able to connect them to others in your network. Remember that we tend to feel compelled to help people who help us. Be a connector of people.

Thomas Power, the Chairman of online network Ecademy, says that "connectivity equals attractiveness." Thomas believes that the more you are able to connect people, the more useful introductions you make for them, then the more attractive you are to them. That makes perfect sense.

I was attending a networking event in Gerrards Cross, in Buckinghamshire, a few years ago. The woman I was speaking to told me that she specialised in online marketing. I asked her if she would then work with traditional marketing consultants rather than compete with them. She told me that, yes, this was the case.

About twenty minutes later I was talking to someone else who told me that she was a marketing consultant. I asked her if she did any online marketing and if not, would she be interested in meeting someone who did. I then took her across the room and introduced her to the online marketing consultant from earlier.

Later that evening, one of the two marketeers came up to me to thank me for the introduction and to tell me that it promised to be very useful.

My original partner, the online marketer, then stayed in touch with me and asked how she would be able to help me. She also joined her local BRE Group a few days later.

Julia Hubbel, in her networking tips book *When You Schmooze you Lose!* suggests that we 'listen with the intent to serve'. The intent is so important, according to Julia, as "Searching for a way to be of service requires that you listen at all levels while at the same time thinking about what you have to offer. This places the focus purely on the other person and on what you can give."

STAY IN TOUCH

You can carry on demonstrating your interest in people after you have met them at a networking event.

- Send them articles that are relevant to their area of expertise or interest.
- Go back to them for advice, suggestions or feedback.
- Refer them to other people in your network where possible.

Most relationships are built between people who have a genuine interest in each other. One of the strongest ways you can ensure that you stick in people's minds is by showing that you are thinking of them when they least expect it. A common way of doing this is by sending birthday cards, but I think less obvious touches are more likely to make a big impression. Perhaps an enquiry about the health of their family, good luck wishes before a big speech or pitch or even congratulations when their football team wins a big game.

Ideally you should be looking to meet up with people after making contact at networking events. If you network a lot it will be almost impossible to meet with everyone with whom you have established a rapport but certainly aim to meet with the people with whom you have really connected.

Only by meeting up will you really get to know each other and start to build that relationship. In a one–to–one setting outside a networking event, without other people looking to join your conversation, you will have a much greater opportunity to explore each others' business and build your understanding. You will also then be more likely to stick in each others' memory.

To keep the relationship building, invite each other to some of the networking events you will be attending. One former member of BRE, who I originally met at a London Chamber of Commerce event, used to have a policy of doing just this. He would then be 'giving' to them when he met, instead of looking to 'take' and he could easily play the host to them when they attended their next event at his invitation. In a very short time they would be part of his network.

BREAKING OUT OF YOUR COMFORT ZONES

Networking is about moving away from our comfort zones. One of the ways in which we retreat into comfort zones is by focusing our networking and referrals on people whose businesses we find easy to understand, or who may have a close synergy to our own. If you are in a referral–building group and you find yourself doing this, set yourself a goal of asking questions of at least one person whose business you don't understand so well at each meeting you attend. Try to arrange to meet them outside of the regular meeting to find out more about their business. Focus on people who you would like to help but don't know how.

Tell them that you need their help to understand how you can help them and don't be afraid to admit that you are struggling. They should appreciate your honesty and your desire to help them.

MEANING IT

You can't devote all your time to learning about other people's businesses and to helping them. You have a business to run as well. You will find yourself naturally drawn to some people more than others and that is a good sign, you'll find it easier to help people with whom you have an affinity.

If you are going to spend time with people, look to connect them to others and develop a relationship with them. This will strengthen your relationship and will increase the likelihood of them connecting you with people in their network.

You also need to feel comfortable that they will be reliable when you refer them or connect them to other people. Don't offer to help people if you don't mean it, if you don't relate to them or even don't like them. You need to genuinely want to help them.

I went to one networking event recently where the organisers ran a speed networking session. They asked all of the attendees to line up opposite each other and spend three minutes in pairs before changing partners. We were told to ask a question of each other – "How can I help you?"

I found myself asking people who I had never met before how I could help them. It felt completely unnatural. I knew nothing about them or their business and my motivation for asking was not a desire built on rapport and understanding, but the fact that I had been told to ask the question. When I asked the question, I did not feel sincere and I am sure that I would not have come across as sincere.

When I was asked the question by my partners, it was clear from most people's expressions that they were not interested in my answers. They were simply going through the motions as well.

Eventually I did connect a few people to contacts in whom they were interested or who could possibly help them. But that came after we had spoken at length and met up again to find out more about each other – and it was then a pleasure to help them.

What if, after asking questions about the other person and showing an interest in them, they don't reciprocate? Well, ask yourself if they would have shown an interest in you in the first place. If you don't have a rapport with them, you should feel comfortable moving on. All you can do is make sure that you show an interest in others and remember that those who still don't engage are the exceptions who prove the rule – *people are interested in people who are interested in them.*

I find money that people didn't know they had.

TOOL 3 – Ask For What You Want

"The right road lies under your tongue – just ask."
Chinese Proverb

Networking can be fun, it can be very social and it can help you to meet some great friends. We shouldn't lose sight of the fact that, if you are like the vast majority of networkers, you are investing your time and money in networking because you believe that it will help you to grow your business.

If that is the case, somewhere along the line, you are going to be looking for tangible results from your networking activity. As already discussed, you need to know what you want to achieve first and then plan how you are going to get there. A key part of that is helping your networking contacts to understand how they can help you.

AVOIDING PRECONCEPTIONS

At some point, the person to whom you are speaking will ask you what you do. Hopefully, you will already have their interest by focusing on them and showing an interest in their business and their needs as discussed in the previous chapter. However, you can lose that interest in a moment through their preconceptions.

People have preconceptions about everything!

You will probably have had expectations for this book before you read it and an idea of what you wanted to gain from it. Some people will have decided that they didn't want to read it because they feel that they are already skilled networkers while others will devour business books because they perceive that they can always continue developing and learning from them.

At networking events those preconceptions really come into play. As soon as you tell somebody what you do, a little voice in their head makes a decision about your relevance to them. If they do not perceive that what you have to offer is of interest, they will switch off. Accountants, solicitors and financial advisors suffer from this more than most due to the numbers you tend to meet at networking events. Most of us tend to stay with our existing professional contacts, but the problem applies equally to almost everyone, whatever their line of business.

INVITE FURTHER QUESTIONS

Avoid these preconceptions by responding to the question "What do you do?" in a way that invites further questions rather than switching people off. Tell people how you help your clients. By that I don't mean the mechanics of what you do but the benefit of your actions.

For example, if you are an accountant, there are several different ways in which you can answer the question "What do you do?"

You could go for the honest and obvious approach of answering the question with a simple "I'm an accountant." The problem with this, as stated above, is that it will immediately switch people off if they are not interested in accountancy or if they do not have a current accounts problem.

If, instead, you focus on an area of your work or the mechanics of it, you can still invite people's judgement, saying instead: "I help my clients to avoid any problems with their tax returns and make sure that their accounts are completed accurately and on time." If you are not focused on your tax return or your accounts at the time of this conversation, what would your response be?

Your response when asked what you need to do needs to stimulate further conversation, to invite people to want to hear more. When you have answered it should be unavoidable for people to ask a further question, such as "How do you do that?" or "Does that mean you...?"

For our accountant, you might answer that you help your clients focus on their core business or help people to enjoy their work. When asked to elaborate, you can explain how people don't tend to go into business to worry about tax returns or accounts. By relying on someone who does enjoy that side of business, they can focus on the part of the business that they are passionate about, their core business.

This brings to life the benefits of having an accountant, not the mechanics of completing tax returns but the freedom it offers you, so you can focus on other areas.

Try to avoid sounding too clichéd when you answer, you need your response to sound interesting, not scripted. The end result though, is that the person you are speaking to is almost compelled to ask a question as a result, such as "How do you do that?" thereby engaging them in a conversation.

BE PASSIONATE

If you are not passionate about your business, how can you expect anyone else to be? To make an impact; for people to want to know more; to ensure that others really believe that you are the person to speak to or refer in your field, you need to inspire them through your enthusiasm and passion.

If you can enthuse people with your passion they will be drawn to you. As Nigel Risner, author of *You Had Me at 'Hello'* says "People buy passion, not products."

When you talk about what you do, talk with conviction, with belief and with a smile on your lips and sparkle in your eye. When someone asks you a question, give a considered response rather than a mechanical one. Give alternatives and be generous with your advice and support where possible. Remember the impact that you will make if you help someone without expecting anything in return.

Richard Agarwala was a member of the first ever BRE Group in Potters Bar in Hertfordshire in 1999. Richard was a Partner in the legal firm of Male and Wagland and used to talk about all aspects of the law.

For many people in business, hearing a solicitor speak about the intricacies of conveyancing, employment tribunals or divorce does not tend to be the highlight of their day, let alone their week. However, Richard's sixty second presentations each week were eagerly anticipated by all of the members. He delivered a wonderful blend of humour, passion and belief culminating in a great story.

Richard didn't just entertain, however. Members of the Group learnt about his business, how he helped his clients and the type of referrals he was looking for through his stories. The first year of their membership resulted in over £100,000 worth of fee income for Male and Wagland, in no small part because of the impact Richard made with his presentations.

DON'T BE A 'LONER'

As Mike Southon says in *The Beermat Entrepreneur*, "Entrepreneurs truly change the world. But they don't do so alone." A key mindset to lose before you go to networking events is the 'loner mentality'. Loners are people who either don't feel worthy of other people's help or feel that they can achieve their ambitions without the help of others. If you feel like that then people are going to find it very difficult to help you and you will struggle to get benefits from your networking.

It is important to understand that you are but one cog in the wheel of commerce and industry. We need to do our bit and everyone else to do theirs if the machine is going to operate effectively and this is the basis on which networking works.

The 'Loner Mentality' will get in your way to success through networking. Other people can help you when you need support, information or just need to discuss ideas and see how realistic your plans are.

Instead of being self–reliant, be as open to the prospect of other people helping you as you now are to the opportunities to help others. Be aware of when people may be in a position to help and who their connections are. With that awareness, when people want to help, you can help them to understand how they can do so effectively.

TIMING

According to Robert Cialdini, the author of *Influence: The Psychology of Persuasion*, there are 'moments of power' in the relationship between two people, when you have the most influence. It is important to be aware of these if you want to be in a position to accept the opportunities offered by people who want to help you.

When would you be more likely to want to help me and to make sure that you followed through;

- When you have just met me and we've enjoyed a five minute conversation at a networking event?
- When we have just spent an hour together discussing your business at my invitation?
- When you've just heard from me because a mutual contact gave me your name?
- When we've had a social evening together after a year of friendship?

Timing plays an important role in asking for what you want, particularly if the contact you are looking for is a valued one or a connection that can only be made once.

Cialdini tells us that the most powerful moment is when someone has just said 'thank you' for something you have done for them. All too often we dismiss this with 'it was nothing' or 'don't worry about it'. In that instant we have trivialised what we have done when, quite probably, it wasn't 'nothing', for us or for the recipient. We have also lost our 'moment of power' when the other person was most likely to help us.

An obligation to respond in kind has been taught to us from childhood and we are always looking for ways in which we can help people who help us. This is why Ivan Misner's 'Givers Gain' concept, where the people who give the most in a network gain the most from it, works so well. While we shouldn't jump on everybody who says 'thank you' with a *quid pro quo*, we do need to be aware of the best time to ask people for help when we need it.

IT'S HOW YOU ASK

It is vitally important that you think about the way you ask for help as well as just the timing of it. You can risk alienating friends and destroying relationships if you ask in the wrong way.

As we will shortly be discussing, your requests should be clear and concise and easy for the other person to both digest and act upon.

It should also be empowering rather than demanding, ensuring that the other person is delighted to help you rather than feeling put on the spot or under pressure.

Robert Clay, of the Milton Keynes based marketing company DSP Communications, offers examples of effective and ineffective requests for support:

Demanding: "I need you to give me..."

vs

Empowering: "I am looking for ... and thought you might..."

Manipulative: "If you will...I will..."

vs

Empowering: "I have some people to refer to you... and please keep me in mind when you meet people who..."

Hesitant: "I know you're busy and probably won't have time and I don't want to bother you, but..."

vs

Straightforward: "I would like your assistance, if possible. Any amount of time you could give me will be appreciated."

As Robert says, "If you make demands rather than requests, you're just setting yourself up for disappointment."

SPELL IT OUT

When people ask how they can help you, help them by asking for what you want and making it easy for them to understand how they can be of assistance. Our culture sometimes tells us that it is rude to ask for things, we should wait until they are offered. However, I am a great believer that, if you don't ask, you don't get.

Don't expect your networking contacts to be mind readers. Communicate very clearly the contacts of value to you, the clients you are looking for, and the help you need. So many companies recognise the value of referrals and recommendations to their business but don't do anything about it.

One firm of accountants who joined BRE in London wrote to their clients and asked them a simple question, "Would you be happy to recommend us to any of your contacts who need a new accountant?" 80% of the people they wrote to replied, all confirming that they would be more than happy to do so. Until that point, the firm had not been receiving many referrals from their clients at all. Why? They had never asked.

PAINT A PICTURE

Let your network know what you do, who you do it for and how you benefit your clients. Make sure that they understand your business in as much depth as possible. People who attend referral groups and who stand up each week and say what they do often don't understand why they don't receive the quality of referrals they are looking for. The reason is that they are not giving their fellow members the right information. They are focusing on the mechanics of their business and not the benefits.

You need to be able to paint a picture for people. People need to know:

- Who you want to talk to?
- How they can recognise them?
- Why they would want to talk to you?
- How you can help them?

I have heard Financial Advisors ask to be introduced to 'High net–worth individuals'. Speak simple language that others can understand. If they had asked to be introduced to people who live in a certain affluent borough or people who drive high performance or luxury cars, they would have made it much easier for the others in their group to recognise their potential clients. Paint a picture to help people recognise their own contacts.

Don't be afraid to be specific. The clearer and more focused the picture you paint; the more likely it is that people will be able to make the connection for you.

Stephen Turner, a Facilities Manager in our Croydon East group, stood up one week and asked for a connection in the Wallington office of Canon Copiers. The reason was that the office had a very old fashioned air–conditioning system, which was both unattractive and inefficient and Stephen said that he could modernise it and provide both a better working environment and cost savings.

On hearing Stephen's request, another member of the group replied that he had worked for Canon for eighteen years and had spent eleven years in the Wallington office. He would be happy to go back to his old contacts and try to provide the introduction that Stephen was looking for.

If Stephen's request had been more general, for companies with outdated air conditioning systems, the chances are that the visitor would not have made the connection and recognised his former workplace. The opportunity would have been lost.

HOW DO YOU EAT AN ELEPHANT?*

Some people struggle with being specific because they are looking for a wide range of clients for whom they can offer a number of services. In these circumstances, the key is to break down the services you offer or your customer base into bite–size chunks (*this is how you eat an elephant by the way!)

Don't be frightened to focus on just one part of your business when making a request. Would you prefer to ask about your whole business but get no referrals because you haven't been specific enough or focus in on one area of your business and get a connection?

One of our members represented a utilities company. Amongst their services they provide low–cost routing for both domestic and business telecoms. At one breakfast meeting I heard him ask for referrals to "anyone who has a telephone."

Not surprisingly he didn't receive any referrals at the meeting. I asked him to change the presentation for the next meeting and worked with him on the request he was going to make.

At the next meeting he stood up and asked the members present for connections to people who had elderly relatives living on their own but not in care. He received three referrals because he had painted such a specific picture.

WHO DO YOU KNOW WHO...?

As well as being specific, the way that you frame a question can make a big difference to the response you get. Are you looking to limit yourself by only selling to your networking partner? Or are you open to connections into their network?

If the latter is the answer, then you are shutting a very heavy door by just using the term 'you' in your stories and requests. By saying 'if you have this problem', 'if you find yourself in that situation' or 'if you need this', you are not allowing for the possibility that they may not need what you offer but someone they know does.

May I offer you some food for thought here? If you ask people to think about others in their network in a particular situation, if they are in the situation themselves, that will be the first thing to spring to their mind!

In sales much is made of the importance of asking 'open' rather than 'closed' questions, so that you avoid a negative answer. The same rule applies when asking for connections or referrals in networking.

Most people's natural instinct will be to take the easy route. If they cannot think of someone who they know who can help you instantly, they will simply answer 'no' if asked 'do you know anyone who...?' It is important, therefore, that you phrase the question in a different way.

An open question, such as 'who do you know who...?' will make people think. Even if the answer is 'nobody', they have thought more deeply about the question, delving deeper into their network.

PAUSE 'TIL IT .... HURTS

When asking people for their help, it is important that you give them the time to digest your question and think about their response. Many people get very nervous when asking for help and quickly mask their question by carrying on talking, qualifying the question, even explaining that they understand why you *can't* help them. By the time they've finished the other person has forgotten the original request!

One of the best pieces of advice that I ever received about giving presentations was 'pause until it hurts'. Many people are frightened of pauses, in both business and social settings, and will do anything to fill them. Yet they play such an important role in conversation.

If I ask you 'who do you know who...?' I need to give you time to mentally scan your database, think of people who may qualify, ask yourself if they do qualify and cement their picture in your mind before I continue. This may take a matter of just one or two seconds, but that is actually quite a long pause.

How much more effective would my request be if I gave you that time without looking to fill the space the pause presented? Should I then go on to explain why I want the connection you will be thinking of that person and relating my explanation directly to them. This makes it much more likely that you will be happy to make the connection for me.

PROBLEM, SOLUTION, BENEFIT

Once people have got a good idea of who you want to talk to, it is important that they feel comfortable making the connection for you. It will not be sufficient for them to know that you want to speak to Richard Branson, they also need to know why Richard Branson would want to talk to you.

I always suggest putting yourself into the shoes of the person who knows the contact to whom you want to be connected. If they are in a position to help you, how will they make the connection? What will they say to the contact that will make them want to be introduced to you?

A good model to follow when explaining why the connection should be made is 'problem, solution, benefit'. The first question to answer is, "what's the problem?" The American entrepreneur Doug Richard said on the BBC television show *Dragons' Den*, "We all solve problems. You should not be in business if you don't solve problems."

Whoever you want to speak to needs to feel compelled to speak to you. More often than not that will be because they perceive that you can take some pain away or solve a problem for them.

Once you have established that you can solve problems, people will then want to know how. Not in any technical detail, but you do need to get across the solution that you offer and how it is different from anything they have tried before.

Now is the time to underline the benefits of using you and of solving this problem. This really gets to the root of "what's in it for them?"

Using the tools outlined above, a request from the utilities consultant mentioned above would read as follows:

Who do you know who has elderly relatives living alone but not in care?

(PAUSE for long enough so that people start thinking of the elderly people they know)

Money is a major issue for a lot of elderly people living on their pension and they would tend to be very wary of using the telephone because of the cost. Their relatives like to be in constant touch with them to make sure that they are OK and they need to feel confident enough to pick up the phone and ask for help.

We can provide very low cost telephone calls using the major carriers to ensure that there is no fall in call quality.

As a result, relatives can have peace of mind and nobody need to worry about the bills.

TELL A STORY

Once you have all of the pieces of the jigsaw in place you can bring your request to life by giving people case studies to illustrate how you have done this before.

Whenever you are speaking to anyone individually, to a group or giving a presentation, illustrate your point by giving examples from your experience (a bit like we have done in this book). Many people can relate more to what you are saying by visualising what happened to someone else and they are more likely to remember stories than theories or ideas.

People also *like* stories. It makes your request more real and easier to understand. They are also easier to remember and to repeat to others. Most of all, they help to build trust, convincing people that you have done this before, successfully.

Richard White, an expert on 'Soft Selling', says "Elevator speeches are for sales people, stories are for networkers. If you want referrals then stop selling and start telling stories."

Using case studies and anecdotes also make it easier for you to present what you do. It will often be easier for you to use a story to make your explanation clearer and, particularly in presentations, to remember what you are going to say.

We've been doing Presentation Skills training with our BRE Groups. It has been noticeable how people's nerves settle and presentations become more fluent and more expressive when the speaker is recalling instances from their memory rather than trying to read from a script.

So be clear and make sure that you *ask for what you want.*

THREE TECHNIQUES

and conditions of membership.

THE NATIONAL TRUST

30 Apr 06
277 755 560 CD

Mrs A J P L G Tudor
Mr E Tudor

TECHNIQUE 1 – Planning Your Strategy

"Strategy without tactics is the slowest route to victory. Tactics without strategy is the noise before defeat."
Sun Tzu

For many businesses, networking forms the basis of a word of mouth marketing strategy. The aim for most businesses is to build either a larger client base or one of greater quality. People want to be spoken about in a positive way, particularly where opportunities for further business lie.

Like all business strategies, this requires planning and foresight. You need to know what your goals are and how you are going to achieve them.

If you are going to network effectively, you need to understand where, when and how to network. Most importantly, you need to know *why*.

There are an increasing number of networking opportunities available to us including:

- Corporate events such as golf days
- Quarterly and monthly industry or market–specific seminars
- One–off events hosted by private firms
- Regular events by organisations such as the Chambers of Commerce, Federation of Small Businesses and Enterprise Agencies
- Weekly, high commitment breakfast meetings run by organisations like BRE.

Some events promote guest speakers while others allow the participants to do all the talking. You can network at conferences, business exhibitions and at training events. While some organisations are gender–specific, with an increase in the popularity of networking groups for business women.

Don't forget that there are other groups that may be socially based, but can be equally valuable in providing networking opportunities – like Round Table, Rotary Clubs, hobby related groups and similar organisations.

KNOW WHAT YOU WANT TO ACHIEVE

When you decide that you want to join a networking organisation or go to networking events, the first thing that you need to do is to research the different opportunities available to you. Be clear about what you want to achieve. All of these networking organisations operate in slightly different ways and achieve different results.

There are, generally speaking, three types of network:

1. **Brain–Building** organisations typically run seminars or bring together people from similar industries to learn from each other. These play a vital role in helping you to use networking for self–development.

2. **Network–Building** organisations are based around the belief that 'It's not what you know but who you know...and who knows you' and enable participants to meet a wide range of people either at events or online.

   Metcalfe's Law, attributed to Robert Metcalfe, the designer of the Ethernet protocol for computer networks, states that:

   "The usefulness, or utility, of a network equals the square of the number of users."

   The law originally related how technology becomes more effective the more users it has (a fax machine has limited use if you are the only person who has one. The more people who own a fax, the more useful yours becomes). It can, however, be just as easily applied to the power of people networks. The more people to whom you are connected, the easier and more effective your networking becomes.

A successful networker will combine the opportunity to meet new people with developing a network of contacts built around a core of people with whom they have a strong relationship. That relationship is built on increasing trust in each other and a greater understanding of each others' business.

3. **Referral–Building** organisations focus on developing this core of strong relationships, helping members to get to know each other well and build sufficient levels of trust and understanding in each other to both recognise opportunities and to feel comfortable referring them.

The successful networker will know what he or she wants from networking and then decide which organisation(s) meet these objectives. For many this will be a mix of the networks above, rather than one or another. It is then important to decide in which environment you feel the most comfortable.

BUILDING SYNERGIES

Some networking groups, particularly referral focused organisations such as BRE, will exclude membership from competing companies. This becomes very attractive for many organisations that see the potential for new business enhanced by the exclusivity on offer. Such a policy also ensures that a more diverse range of businesses are represented in the membership than may otherwise be the case. The members of such a group can focus on developing relationships and building a real understanding of what each other does instead of trying to out–pitch each other.

There are advantages to finding yourself in a networking group or at an event with one of your competitors. There may be situations, either for geographic reasons or because of your respective strengths and specialities, where it is more beneficial to refer business to each other. This may strengthen the service you offer your clients, and allow you to provide a good service, even if you are very busy or do not have the necessary expertise. This should be a two way street with referrals in both directions. Very often, in such a situation, your competitor can become a key source of new business.

Another area to be aware of is where businesses may have a synergy with yours. They may service clients in a similar position to yours, for example an office removals firm would share a client base with a telecoms company, an office furniture company, a printer and a computer networking company, all of whom help companies moving to new premises.

In the Charlton BRE Group, the Independent Financial Advisor (IFA) in the group brought his accountant along. Within weeks they were sharing a number of referrals on a regular basis.

I asked the IFA if they had been doing this before the accountant had joined the group and the answer was "no"." The focus of the networking group had brought to both of their minds the opportunities to refer their clients to each other, whereas before they had happily worked together without thinking of referrals.

Synergies between companies who meet through networking can also result in the businesses combining to win bigger value contracts than they may have managed on their own. There may also be the opportunity for 'Joint Venture Marketing' groups to be formed as separate companies to pitch for business together.

In the Reading BRE Group, four member companies combined to pitch to Volkswagen Audi. At the time of writing, they had just closed on a pilot with a dealer in Liverpool, with a view to a larger contract should the pilot prove successful.

Paul Voakes of Apollo HR, who is a member of the Reading Group, said that none of the businesses would have been able to pitch for the contract on their own.

"The relationship was only possible because we joined forces to develop a solution with the scope to handle the business issues. We are currently negotiating with a number of larger organisations offering a complete range of services with the core of BRE Reading supplying the solutions. We have a number of opportunities to deliver on this model and believe over the next four months will have delivered two or three, some of which involve eight or nine BRE members."

MEETING YOUR COMMITMENTS

In planning your approach to formal networking, you need to balance these opportunities, work out which organisations suit your needs and to whom you can commit. You should be aware of what is required of you, once you have made that commitment, and be comfortable with that.

If an organisation requires a weekly attendance from you, ensure that you can either meet this commitment or arrange for somebody to represent you in your absence before you decide to join. Remember that if you take on a commitment and are unable to meet it, it is the other members of the group who will be affected. This will not benefit your relationships, or your reputation.

Some events require you to take on responsibilities outside of the meeting, such as a committee position, providing further information or attending meetings with other participants. Make sure that your diary will allow you to meet these demands.

One of the key principles of networking is that everybody will benefit if they are prepared to give. The well–known phrase, 'what goes around, comes around' sums it up beautifully. If you participate in networking only with a view to what you can gain, and so does everyone else, then there is nowhere for the benefits to come from. Networking does, therefore, entail a degree of commitment and sacrifice.

When you have decided upon your networking memberships, making sure that they allow you to both build your network and develop relationships, you need to consider your participation.

MAKING THE MOST OF THE TIME

Most networking events will last for between one and two hours, with some going on for longer if they include guest speakers. That really isn't a great deal of time and so you should endeavour to make the most of it.

Many weekly events take place at breakfast time because the organisers know that this is the best way to guarantee a maximum attendance. For many of us, once we have reached the office, something will always come up, the phone will always ring at the wrong moment and the meeting suddenly becomes a less pressing priority.

Make every effort to turn up at or before the publicised start time and stay on until the end. Plan to start your journey earlier than you need to so you are sure to arrive on time. If you know you have an evening networking event, don't book anything in your diary for early the next morning, allowing you to stay until the end if you are still meeting new people and enjoying interesting conversations.

I always suggest that people leave their diaries clear for a good hour after a networking event is due to end. You can recognise a successful event by the amount of people still around well after the end and the frustrated faces of the organisers as they try to encourage everyone to leave! At one event I attended in Oxford, we were thrown out by the venue after 11pm and the networking carried on for a further quarter of an hour in the car park!

For evening events, if you have a chance, get something to eat beforehand. It can be very uncomfortable enjoying a buffet or canapés while trying to network. It takes a lot of practice shaking someone's hand while holding a prawn sandwich in one hand and a glass of wine in the other. That is without trying to talk with your mouth full! I guarantee that someone will always ask you a question just as you take a big bite!

WHO DO YOU WANT TO TALK TO?

I often get asked whether or not it is advisable to ask for a list of attendees before an event. Many people do and many organisations offer them. If you attend a networking event organised by Ecademy, for example, not only can you click on the website to see a list of attendees, you even get treated to their photographs as well!

There is no simple answer to this question; it really depends on how you plan to use the list. If you want to trawl the list and tick off the people to whom you want to speak, allowing you to seek them out and avoid all others, I would strongly discourage it. Remember the law of Six Degrees of Separation. You could spend your whole event trying to track down people who are not interested in what you offer, while ignoring those who may become your greatest introducers.

I am a great believer in the power of random connections. Pre–planning who you want to speak to limits these opportunities. Not only that, but you will probably find yourself searching through the event for the people who you want to meet only to find them engrossed in conversation and you standing waiting on your own looking and feeling rather foolish! You certainly won't be fully engaged in conversation with other people as you spend half of your time looking to see if your 'target' is free and approachable.

Lists of attendees in advance can be used in a positive way. The photos provided on the Ecademy lists allow me to recognise people with whom I have exchanged emails in the past but have not met before. You may be able to identify someone whom you have wanted to meet or touch base with, but have not yet been able to do so.

In these cases, instead of hunting them out at the event, contact them in advance and arrange to meet either before or afterwards. That way, you establish the relationship that you are looking for without anyone else seeking to join the conversation. You also manage to maximise the networking time available to you to develop new contacts.

SAYING WHAT OTHERS NEED TO HEAR

If you are due to make a presentation, plan and prepare it in advance and ask yourself what impact your words will have on the audience. Will that impact match what you are looking to achieve from the meeting? If not, change your presentation so that it does.

Too often, when we are asked to present our business, we end up saying what we want to say, not what others need to hear. Ask yourself why you are making the presentation. If you do not know the answer, don't do it! If you do, the next step is to ask yourself what other people would need to hear if they are going to help you reach your goal. Or, even better, ask them before you make the presentation.

Remember to ask yourself 'what's the takeaway?' In other words, what will people go away remembering, and telling others about? Make sure that your presentations are both memorable and repeatable.

I have heard so many presentations from businesses who give a broad outline of what they do and then wait for the referrals that never come. The classic line is "You all know what I do." No we don't! No one knows what you do as well as you.

If referrals are your aim, then your audience needs to know not what you do but how to recognise the people who need your help. Why would they need to talk to you? Frequently people say why they want to talk to their target market. I am sorry, but that doesn't help us to make the connection. We need to know what will motivate them to talk to you, not the other way around. Then we need to know what you can do for them and how it will resolve the problem.

As we discussed in an earlier chapter, it is most important for you to say what you want and how you expect people to help you. Say it at the beginning of your presentation and then repeat it at the end so that your audience are left with no doubts as to how they can help you.

> If I was to plan a presentation to encourage further sales of this book and further training opportunities, I might say something like this:
>
> "Who do you know who runs a large sales team?
>
> The chances are that they are working in a very tough market and looking to get ahead of their competitors.

Many organisations rely on traditional sales training and methods but have not yet explored the potential offered by networking events and referral strategies. From this book, through networking training courses and onto membership of BRE Groups, we can help them to tap into the benefits offered by networking and understand how to use it.

This in turn will help them to get ahead of their competitors, who are probably stuck in the office on the telephone!

So, who do you know who runs a large sales team?"

Without *planning your strategy* and knowing what you are trying to achieve and how others can help you, you will struggle to achieve much success from your networking.

TECHNIQUE 2 – Making An Impression

"A thousand words will not leave so deep an impression as one deed."
Henrik Ibsen

I have been to networking breakfasts, networking lunches and networking dinners. I have even spoken at a charity 'Networkathon', a 24–hour networking event run by a group in Chelmsford, Essex. With so many events available to us and with up to two hundred people attending individual networking meetings, it can become harder and harder to stand out from the crowd. If you want people at these events to not only remember you, but also to want to pursue a relationship with you afterwards, it is vital that you can make a positive impression upon them.

You can do this both in the way you interact with individuals at the event and through the role you take in the event itself. Start off by going along to an event and asking yourself who has made an impression on you and then look at what they have done that is different to everybody else there.

- Why is it that they spring to mind?
- What made them different to the other people who you met?

We have already looked at the importance of showing an interest in other people, being curious and being in the room for them when you are in conversation. Ensure that you do this and maintain constant and positive eye contact with the other people with whom you are speaking and you will have a head start on others.

MAKE AN IMPACT

The first step is to make the right sort of impact when you first meet people and introduce your business to them.

According to Lesley Everett, author of *Walking TALL*, "The majority of the first impression is based on non–verbal communication, that is our appearance and body indicators. Every message needs a medium to present it with impact – your messages of personal values, standards, abilities – in fact what you stand for – will be strongly projected through your personal image and how you present yourself."

It doesn't matter what you are going to say or how much you listen if you haven't made the right impression in the first place. If you haven't done so already, it can be worth asking a Personal Impact Coach like Lesley or an image consultant to spend time with you. This will make sure that you are getting across the right message through your image.

Make sure that you look the part, are professionally turned out and sober. That does not necessarily mean that you have to wear a business suit to all networking groups that you attend. It is fine to be dressed according to what is appropriate to both your profession and the environment you're networking in. You can, however, still appear smart and professional within those standards or scruffy and unprofessional. As Lesley goes on to say, "Grooming and clothes are the 'packaging' of your total image and speak volumes about your values and personal brand."

Gus Paul is a builder who joined BRE in Borehamwood, Hertfordshire a few years ago. When Gus first came along to meetings he always wore a suit, shirt and tie. After the meeting had finished Gus would then go home and get changed into his work clothes before going to his first appointment. As a result, he was losing up to an hour a week when he could have been working.

When the members of the Group discovered what Gus had been doing they persuaded him that he did not need to wear a suit and he should wear what he was comfortable in and what would allow him to go onto work straight from the meeting.

Gus turned up for the next meeting smartly dressed in casual clothes, with his overalls waiting for him in his van for his first job after the meeting. As a result he felt much more comfortable in the meetings and less out of place.

A big trap at a lot of networking events is the free alcohol on offer. I will rarely drink while I am networking and almost never in the first hour of an event. At one event one of the attendees enjoyed the wine being freely served a little too much. By half way through the event he was slurring his words badly, his breath reeked of white wine and he was generally making a fool of himself. He did a lot of damage to his reputation that evening and even though this was some years ago, a lot of people who were present still remember him for that.

When you introduce yourself to someone new, don't underestimate the power of a smile and warmth. Remember that many people you meet will be very nervous and ill at ease and, if you are friendly, you will make a very positive impact on them.

BE POSITIVE

It is so important for you to represent the image you want for your company at all times while you are networking.

> I remember one breakfast meeting where I was greeting people as they came in. One member of the group walked in quite late and we started chatting.
>
> I couldn't believe the frame of mind that this woman carried into the meeting. She complained of being tired, of needing her coffee, how she had not yet woken up, even of how she had put her back out the week before by sneezing! She did not have one positive word to say. Naturally I was glad to move on from that conversation!
>
> Ten minutes later, I needed to speak to the same member. I walked over to the group where she was in conversation and waited for the opportunity to catch her attention. I was amazed at what I heard.
>
> The same person, who shortly before had been complaining to me about how she was feeling, was discussing one of her clients. The client was suffering from cancer and the member was explaining how she had been encouraging her client to develop a more positive frame of mind, how constantly talking about the cancer would worsen the symptoms.
>
> The member was a life coach and encourages her clients to have a positive frame of mind. Yet her frame of mind at that meeting had been anything but positive. She had completely failed to sell herself as a coach in those few minutes with me at the start of the event.

The old adage of 'Do as I say, not what I do' does not carry any weight at networking events.

REMEMBERING NAMES

In *How to Win Friends and Influence People*, Dale Carnegie told us to 'Remember that a person's name is, to that person, the sweetest and most important sound in any language'. People like to be remembered and showing that you are interested in their name is the first indication that you are going to show an interest in that person.

When someone introduces themselves to you, listen to what they are saying carefully and make the effort to *hear* their name when it is spoken. You can then repeat it to make sure that you have heard it correctly, and imprint it on your memory.

"I'm sorry, is that Michael? Hello Michael, it's nice to meet you."

If they have already handed you their business card, look at the name on the card as well as this will reinforce it for you.

Try to use the other person's name in conversation as much as is naturally possible. Not only will appropriate repetition of their name make a positive impression on others, it will help you to remember their name in the future. When the conversation ends, say their name again as you bid each other farewell.

If you can remember people's names the next time you meet them, together with where you met them previously and something about them, they will feel flattered. Subsequently they will be more likely to relax in your company and the relationship will be easier to build. This is another area where writing on the back of business cards will help you.

When you are visiting an event for a second time, look through the contacts that you made on your last visit and, if available, the list of people attending. If you know who you are likely to meet for the second time, you will be more prepared when you see them again.

While you should do as much as possible to help yourself to remember names, do not worry if you are unable to. Many people struggle to remember the names of people who they have met several times, let alone those of the people who they have only met once or twice! There can be a strong temptation to avoid potential embarrassment by not going up to people at events when we feel that we should know their name, but can't remember.

If you take this 'easy' road out you may be missing out on a valuable opportunity. It is very unlikely that people will be offended if you approach them with an apology for forgetting their name. They may well have forgotten yours as well! Honesty tends to be respected in networking environments, just make sure that you try to remember their name the next time you meet!

Introduce yourself first with your name, making the other person feel more comfortable, and help others to remember your name by saying it clearly, particularly if you have an unusual first or last name. After all, if people can remember your name it is likely that it will be easier for them to recall other key facts about you. Take equal care when introducing the name of your company or details of what you do.

WEARING BADGES

If you wear a badge with your name written clearly on it will help people to overcome any memory lapses. Many people use their business card as a badge when they attend networking events. The problem with this is that business cards are not designed with this use in mind. The writing is often too small to read easily and the peripheral information, such as your contact address and numbers, detract from your name and company name, making it difficult for these key items to stand out when worn as a badge.

Invest a few pennies in producing a smart badge that is both clear and professional. You can guarantee that you will stand out from many others present at the networking event. By wearing this at an event you will also be advertising your own company logo rather than that of the host.

If you do not like putting badge pins through your suits and have nowhere to put a clip badge, you can now purchase magnetic badges with a separate back that sits behind your clothing. If you wear the badge high on the right hand side of your jacket or top it will be in the direct eye line of the person with whom you are shaking hands.

FEELING CROWDED?

One of the biggest mistakes that you can make at networking events is to get too close to your partner. Everyone has their own personal space and, even if you are comfortable ‘up close and personal', remember that networking is about the other person. Be aware of where they are comfortable in relation to you.

Personal space varies from person to person but generally in Western society you will not be too intimate if you stand around three feet away from your partner. Any further and they may worry that you are too distant, or you may find yourself shouting to each other as people push between you!

If you are getting too close, people will generally take a step backwards to reset the distance between you. Be conscious of this and respect their wish without feeling offended. Don't start trying to close the distance between you; this could be taken either as very aggressive or as an unwelcome proposition. Similarly, if you feel that your space is being invaded, take a gentle step backwards, or alter the angle between you so that you are not face–to–face.

NETWORKING WITH DIFFERENT SEXES

Many networks, ours included, suffer from a poor representation by women amongst their membership. As a result many networking events are male dominated and women–only networks are growing in popularity.

This is something that we are keen to reverse. The more male–dominated events become, the less attractive they are for women to attend and the problem, subsequently, becomes worse. In general (and I accept that this is a generalisation), women are much better listeners than men and tend to be more alert to connections that they can make. Networks would undoubtedly benefit from a better gender balance.

In an article for the Daily Telegraph in November 2005, Etta Cohen of Forward Ladies in Leeds said, "Women behave differently when men are not there. It's more relaxed. Women spend more time getting to know people.

"Men will concentrate more on 'We have come together for business, what is your business?' Women will talk more about family, clothes, holidays. It's not that they are not business focused, but they want to get to know people. Every lady comes to this network to do business. But they want to do it in an environment where they don't feel threatened."

It is important to be aware of the key differences in how men and women communicate when networking with people of the opposite sex, as this will drive the way they approach such events. Men will often look to dominate conversations and bring them around to their point of view, while women look to be more inclusive.

Mary E. Hughes, in her presentation *Gender Differences in Communication*, said, "Some of the differences in communication styles between men and women reflect general differences in their world views. For men, conversations are negotiations and reflect who is in charge, who is right, and who knows the answers. For women, conversations are opportunities to be close, to connect with others, to create a network, and to maintain relationships."

Interestingly, the Australian feminist and author Dale Spender has run a number of studies on this issue. In her book *Man Made Language* she taped people's conversations and discovered women: "asked the right questions, provided encouragement and feedback, made the male speaker feel important. But this meant that men did most of the talking.

"Women who did talk for more than about one third of the conversation were most often described as bossy, aggressive, rude, and as dominating the conversation, even when they got much less than a 50 per cent share."

In another study, Dale found that men interrupt 98% more than women and men generally define a good conversation as one where they held the floor, while women generally define a good conversation as one where everyone had a turn.

Once you have a strong understanding of the different way men and women approach networking, approach conversations and interact in a group, you should be better able to adapt the away you participate.

There is a clear responsibility for event organisers to address key issues such as the time and location of the meetings to encourage more women to attend. Everyone present also shares the burden of responsibility, ensuring that the overriding focus of everyone present is 'getting to know people'.

Many people feel strongly that men should treat women in exactly the same way that they would treat other men in business. I agree with this view, to a point. While traditional courtesy, such as opening a door, should not be out of place, too much attention paid to the other person's gender can be counter productive. In the very worst scenarios you risk being seen as 'slimy' or your behaviour as inappropriate.

Where I disagree with the point of view above is that it does not allow for women's feelings on attending male–dominated events. Where men congregate in groups it can be daunting for women to 'break in' to the group. The same is true for men attending women's networking events, as I have done in the past, and it is important to be aware of such feelings and ensure that you are welcoming.

If you are female, new to networking and are daunted by the prospect of going to a male–dominated event, there are two positive steps you can take to ease the fear. You can start by going to women–only events to get used to networking and presenting and build your confidence. These events are excellent and well–worth attending but, depending on your networking strategy, I would suggest looking to attend other events as well.

On attending non gender–specific events, make sure that you go with one or more friends or colleagues. When you enter the room you will not feel so intimidated and will find it easier to get into the flow of the event and build the confidence to meet new people.

When speaking to someone of the opposite sex, you should be even more aware of their personal space as you might be otherwise. Again, it is important that your actions are not seen as inappropriate or your motives questioned.

In a discussion I initiated on this subject on Ecademy, one of the participants, William Buist identified the problem very clearly. "The responsibility for being inclusive is ours as individuals because only we control how inclusive we want to be. You can't win by sharing if you don't include some of the people you should be sharing with."

BEING HEARD

I find that I have a head start at many of the events I attend because I take the opportunity to give a presentation at them. By being seen as an expert in your field, people are more likely to want to know you and to learn from you. We have already seen how important it is to overcome the fear of speaking in public. If you can overcome this fear you will find yourself with a valuable tool in your marketing armoury.

To conquer this fear and to develop your public speaking skills, after reading the section on speaking in public in this book, I would suggest that you find out where your local Toastmasters group or Public Speaking Club is. These clubs can be found across the globe and membership tends to be inexpensive. They are built around a structure designed to enhance their members' ability to present in public and many of them, such as Toastmasters, offer a system of accreditation allowing you to develop along a recognised route.

When you feel that you have the confidence in your ability, look out for opportunities to speak at networking events. Start at groups where you are a member, it is often easier to present to people who you already know. Many local groups are always looking out for business speakers who are willing to share their expertise with their members. Just remember that people want to learn from you, not be pitched at. Avoid giving an advertisement for your company, instead look to ensure that the audience goes away with knowledge that they didn't have when they arrived.

If you want to capitalise on these opportunities, you should ensure that you do not rush off as soon as possible after your talk. Try to stay until the end of the meeting to give people the chance to come and speak to you and ask you questions. At this stage you will have people's interest and you need to be there to capitalise on it.

I will also often ask the organisers if I can give the audience a feedback form to fill out after my talk. This gives me a valuable insight to the impact I have had on the audience and ideas to improve my presentation. Many people who fill these forms out are happy to give me their contact details and welcome a follow–up. I always try to ensure that I follow up the forms with a simple email within a couple of days of the event and this gives me the opportunity to build a relationship with the people who respond to my emails.

BE READY FOR THE OPPORTUNITY TO SPEAK

If you do not feel that you have the confidence or inclination to present a full scale talk, there are still many opportunities to speak at networking events. Many events now offer the opportunity to all attendees to present, while others offer 'a minute to win it' slot where a small number of attendees are given this opportunity.

Be prepared for these opportunities to come up by having a presentation ready in your mind. Ensure that you are able to convey a clear message about your business, in less than one minute, which people will respond to.

Ask clients and colleagues what they think you should say in that time. Rehearse presentations to them, to your family or even to your dog or cat so that when you go along to the event you feel comfortable with what you are going to say.

Try not to read from a script – it will make your presentation sound uninteresting and dry. As soon as you start reading it is likely that you will lose all expression and animation and people will switch off. You may use index cards with bullet points to prompt you if you feel you need something to guide you. Give yourself a series of headlines or questions that you can answer.

After all, when people ask you a question about your business, you don't need to read them the reply. Do you?

If you want to build a strong network of people who will pick up the phone when you call, read your emails when you send them and help you when you can, it is vital that you *make an impression* when you first meet them.

TECHNIQUE 3 – Keeping In Touch

"You may admire a girl's curves on the first introduction, but the second meeting shows up new angles."
Mae West

Possibly the most difficult skill in networking effectively is the ability to keep in touch with people after the event and build relationships over a period of time. Without ensuring that we do this well, the rest of our time has been wasted. Robert Clay puts it beautifully when he says, "A connection is just like a package you receive. You don't know whether the package contains gold, silver or paper until you take the time to unwrap it and discover what is inside."

The old 9am–5pm work day and five day working week is disappearing as more and more people leave corporate life and work for themselves or in smaller companies. Even in larger companies, employees are putting in extra hours, working from home and operating on flexitime as workforces are downsized and the work mounts. With networking events taking up mornings, lunches and evenings as well, time spent in the office at our desks becomes more and more precious.

However, we can't afford to allow the lack of time available to affect the efforts made to keep in touch with our networking contacts. As Nigel Risner, author of *You Had Me at 'Hello'* said, "In golf, as in networking, it's the follow–through that counts." People will judge you as much on the effectiveness of your follow–up as on your skills as a conversationalist. You may get the basics right in the meeting but you can destroy all of your hard work by proving to be unreliable after the event.

KEEPING RECORDS

Dedicate time in the office after each event to make sure that you review the business cards that you received and take the appropriate action. Keep a database of the people who you meet, you can either build a simple database in Microsoft Access or similar programmes, or buy a Contact Management System such as Act or Goldmine.

Make sure that you enter the details of your new contacts at the earliest possible opportunity. Otherwise you end up with a pile of business cards on your desk and an ever–more arduous task of inputting the details and remembering what you said and what you promised. This becomes a task that you will keep putting off until the contacts have gone cold. I find that I am always more energised and motivated to record the details immediately after an event than a couple of weeks later when I am struggling to recollect the conversation.

As well as recording your new contact's information in your database, many management systems, notably Microsoft Outlook, allow you to create an electronic version of your business card. You can attach this to any emails that you send, which makes it easier for others to capture and keep your information.

NO EXCUSES

The same fears and excuses that hold us back from attending events or approaching people can also affect our follow–up. From prioritising other business, belief that nothing will come from the contact to the conviction that the other person will not want to hear from us, we can always find ways to rationalise our inaction.

These naturally become self–fulfilling prophecies and the easiest way to avoid that is to ignore them and follow up anyway. If you send one email and it is not returned, what has the cost been to you?

If you prevaricate before following up because you are worried that your approach will be rejected, ask yourself why your contact gave you their card in the first place. If you collected their card because you had a positive conversation, then why would they not want to build on that? If you left with a positive course of action to follow, why should they not want to hear from you?

DON'T SEND JUNK

The follow–up needs to be effective and relevant. People aren't going to thank you if you use their card simply to add them to your mailing list for promotional offers and newsletters. They will be even less receptive to receiving emails with large attachments or heavy brochures through the post if they haven't requested them. If you do feel it would be appropriate to send publicity or sales material, tell them why you would like to do so and ask for their permission.

The worst way in which to follow up people from a networking event is to send unsolicited emails to everyone on the attendee list. This really doesn't go down very well and organisers frequently receive complaints when this happens.

How would you feel if you went to an event and everyone took this approach? If there were two hundred people at the event and the next day you received two hundred unsolicited emails and letters from companies, many of whom you didn't meet, I would hazard a guess that you probably wouldn't be too happy.

Follow up the people with whom you have made a genuine connection or, occasionally, people who you wanted to meet at the event but didn't have the opportunity to do so. If you take the latter course, explain why you wanted to meet them and why you want to make the contact. If you want to ensure that they will acknowledge and respond to your approach the same rules of engagement apply, tell them why you are interested in them, rather than how they can help you.

I normally follow contacts up in the first instance with a short email acknowledging our meeting and any follow–up actions that we agreed. If I have promised to connect them to somebody else in my network, I will do so as early as possible by copying both in on an email explaining the reasons for the connection. If necessary this would be preceded by any appropriate telephone calls.

I never attempt to use my emails to sell to the other person. If they have asked for information I will provide the answers and leave the other person to make their own decision. If they haven't

I won't burden them. I always include a 'signature' on my email which includes a link to our website, giving the other person the opportunity to find out more if they so choose.

If you spend a lot of time travelling and the follow–ups tend to mount up by the time you have got back to the office, it may be an idea to take a leaf from Nigel Risner's book.

Nigel speaks worldwide and finds it difficult to follow people up punctually by email. Instead, Nigel carries around with him a set of his own postcards which he can write a note on and send the next day. He finds that this makes his life easier and makes a great impression on the people he sends them to.

AFTER THE FIRST FOLLOW–UP

Once you have made the initial connection after the event it is important to stay in touch if you are going to build a relationship. Remember that people are interested in people who are interested in them. The more you can show that you are thinking about the other person, the more they will become a friend and valuable contact who will promote your business.

I received an email from a fellow speaker in November 2003 after I had first sent a good luck message and then congratulations to a mutual friend, Tracy Plaice, who was performing on the piano at the national conference of the Professional Speaker's Association. This was a major event for Tracy as she was overcoming a long–time fear of performing in public.

Jo's email said:

"Just wanted to say you are amazing the way you remember what everyone is up to and wish them luck. Tracy was stunned you returned her text at 2am!!"

If you know what is happening in people's lives, what is important to them and when it is happening and wish them good luck or ask how things went it makes so much difference and doesn't require a lot of time or effort. Make yourself available for support or advice if it is needed. By doing this you will accelerate your relationships and build a team of people who will be there for you when you need their help or support.

Look out for articles in magazines or messages in online forums that may be of interest to your contacts and send them a copy or a link. Again, you are demonstrating how you are thinking of them even if there is no firm action to take at that time.

Most importantly, connect people to others in your network whenever you can. Whether it is potential customers, people in a similar line of work, someone interested in attending a course or simply someone who needs advice, if you can keep connecting people both parties will generally appreciate it.

On a regular basis trawl your contact management system and reconnect with people with whom you haven't been in touch for some time.

According to Jan Vermeiren, research has shown that, in order to stay at the top of a contact's mind, you need to connect with them at least as regularly as every six months once you have firmly established your relationship. The initial exchanges should be more frequent, with Jan suggesting four interactions within a month of your first meeting.

WRITING THE NEWS

An increasing number of businesses are now choosing to keep in touch with people through a regular email newsletter. You need to put careful thought into how you are going to do this if you choose to use this medium. Without proper planning and thought your newsletter may be seen as an irritant rather than welcomed.

The last statistic I heard was that it is estimated that 60% of all email traffic is 'spam' or unsolicited emails. While the majority of this spam may be pornographic in nature or offering you certain cosmetic enhancements, I know that I am receiving an ever–growing amount of business newsletters from people who I do not remember ever meeting and certainly haven't requested further information from. On the whole these tend to be deleted without being read as I simply do not have the time to read them all.

Having said that, newsletters can be both welcome and effective in helping to keep you in people's minds. The American speaker, Susan Keane Baker, recently recounted in an interview how she likes a cartoon of Santa Claus at home in the North Pole. Looking in his mailbox, Santa is disappointed to find no Valentine Cards for him.

"No matter how great you are in one season," said Susan, "people will forget you. So the newsletter is just a great no pressure way for me to stay in touch with people."

I try to read the email newsletters that I have requested specifically for the content or from people whom I know well. Many newsletters are beautifully designed offering lots of links to different articles of interest, but the best ones I receive are short and sweet, with one key point that I can take from them and then move on.

The ideal newsletter for me would be one I had chosen to receive that is less than a page of A4 long if printed out and arrives just once a month. In this way the sender makes a greater and more positive impact than somebody sending an email with several links every week, which I don't have the time to read.

A lot of people have mentioned to me that they prefer e–newsletters that are written personally rather than heavily formatted as obvious vehicles to up sell. They feel that they can tell when someone enjoys writing or not, and that enjoyment is infectious.

If you want to start a newsletter or add new contacts to an existing mailing list, ask for their permission first. If you have made a genuine connection with them, it is unlikely that they will refuse and if they do at least you know that you need to do something different to stay in touch with them. You may have fewer subscribers, but at least a larger proportion of the people who do subscribe will read the newsletter.

PICK UP THE PHONE AND MEET IN PERSON

As email has grown into by far and away the prime communication medium for modern business, it has become easier to ignore the traditional methods of speaking, in person or by telephone.

By just staying in touch with people by email, you will become a 'virtual' personality to your connections and they will forget why you built a rapport in the first place.

Take the time to reconnect by picking up the phone, arranging to meet for a drink when you are close to them and just chatting. You don't always need an agenda to meet with or speak to people. Make the effort to stay in touch whenever you can.

When you are going back to networking events that you have attended before, use the opportunity to add more building blocks to the relationship with people who you met there on a previous occasion. If you know that they are going to attend, drop them an email or give them a call in advance to arrange to meet. Perhaps clear some time either before or after the event to sit down and chat rather than doing so during the event itself.

ASK FOR FEEDBACK

Once you have made an introduction or passed a referral or some information to a contact, ask them for some feedback. Was this the sort of thing that was of use to them? Did anything result from the introduction? If not, is there anything you should know to make future connections more successful?

By doing this you are continuing to show interest in your contact and, at the same time, putting your mind at rest about their reliability. By discussing the connection you have made you will be increasing the possibilities of being able to make similar, or better, connections in the future. You will also be able to find more ideas to prompt you to be able to help your contact or other people in your network.

In addition to this, if the connection or information you have passed has been beneficial to your new contact, you will be putting yourself into a prime position to ask for their help.

However you choose to do so, *keep in touch* with the people you meet at networking events. Seek to develop a network of people who you are always looking to support and who are there to support you.

Networking Effectively

So, there you have it; three tips, three tools and three techniques to help you network and make the room work for you.

- Be courageous,
- Be committed,
- ... and be patient.

- Pursue the relationship, not the sale.
- People are interested in people who are interested in them.
- Ask for what you want.

- Plan your networking strategy.
- Make an impression.
- Keep in touch with the people who you meet.

Many people enjoy saying, “It’s not what you know, it’s who you know” when describing how contacts can bring you success. But how accurate is that statement?

Often it is not enough for you to know key people who can connect you, but you need them to know you. The two concepts are very different.

They need to know you well enough to trust you, to want to help you and to understand your personal or business needs in depth. Enough depth to recognise opportunities for you when they arise, whether or not you are present or are aware of the opportunities yourself.

Therefore, it’s not what you know, nor is it who you know, that really makes the difference. It’s *who knows you* that is the key to achieving success, and that’s where networking plays such an important role.

Networking can be great fun and provide so many benefits to you both personally and to your business. The key to that success lies in knowing what you are doing and why you are doing it.

Remember, sow the seeds of successful relationships and you will reap the rewards over time.

"If you want a successful business in one year, grow wheat. If you want a successful business in ten years, grow trees. But if you want a successful business for life, grow people."
source unknown

Andy Lopata

THE ART OF SPEAKING IN PUBLIC

The tips, tools & techniques to help you
stand up and speak with confidence

What's So Important About Being Able To Speak In Public?

I believe speaking is so emotive because the subject is based upon our childhood experiences.

Up to the age of five most children are forever talking and asking 'why?' – at least my three were! Yet when children go to school they suddenly have to be quiet and 'speak when they are spoken to'.

There was a little boy who was trying to speak to his parents – they were talking to a group of grown ups. He was trying to get their attention and interrupted their conversation. Finally, exasperated with the boy, his mother said, "Please be quiet, people are talking..."

The boy, looking very upset and near to tears, said "But I'm people too."

We are not born with the fear of speaking, but for many young people, by the time they have left school or college most have an aversion to speaking up for themselves. This is often because they've been continually told to be quiet, or made fun of by their mates when they've spoken up.

Yet in business at some point that fear has to be overcome if we are to present ourselves professionally.

But how seriously do we take this?

I was at a networking meeting one morning and found myself sitting next to the Group Purchasing Director of a FTSE 100 company. We found we had common ground based upon my experience in corporate life in the Eighties and Nineties. I asked him how many suppliers he replaced annually – apparently around 35 against a book of several hundred.

I asked him the key criteria he and his department used to measure these suppliers and he said that there were five keys – Price, Availability, Track Record, Relationship and Presentation.

His statistics showed that 81% of organisations were poor at presentation.

Only 19% were acceptable, in other words, roughly one in five.

So four out of five presentations were unacceptable – what a waste of time and money for all!

In other words four out of five Business presentations fail.

Incidentally, the numbers for relationships were even worse – his figures showed conclusively that 90% of organisations were incapable of creating long–term relationships, which are vital for his business!

I asked a simple question, "How many of the people that gave a poor presentation, in other words, the 81%, do you actually tell? You know, give them feedback?"

He had a wry smile on his face and said, "Don't be daft I'm British!"

In a nutshell he explained what I always knew. In my corporate career I'd had many sales teams reporting to me and each month we would assess where business was coming from and why we hadn't created new business with prospective clients.

Whilst I heard every story regarding price, availability, competitiveness, dealing with old friends and so on, no–one ever told me they gave a poor presentation!

Including me!

These days when I have finished a speech it's common for people to come and speak to me afterwards and, thankfully, they usually have good things to say!

However, increasingly there is at least one person that comes and chats. The story is usually along the lines that they enjoyed the talk and admire how I can speak to large audiences, however, in their job or business, they don't have the same needs as most times it's a presentation to just a couple of people – and that they usually are pretty good at it!

I always say "well done," yet inside I think 'HOW DO YOU KNOW?'

Four out of five business presentations are unacceptable – how much business is he losing?

And if you make presentations – HOW MUCH IS IT COSTING YOU OR YOUR BUSINESS?

If you doubled your success rate what would that do for you?

But how easy is it to do this?

I'm very lucky and privileged to have been a Regional President and Fellow of the PSA (Professional Speakers Association), which means I see an awful lot of professional speakers. Although many are fantastic and can hold an audience in the palm of their hands, they're not my favourite speakers.

My favourite speaker is typically a charity co–ordinator, who works with their charity as a volunteer because they're passionate about the cause. They probably also have a day job.

One day someone says "Could you just do five minutes for us before we give you the cheque?" All of a sudden they're thrust into the limelight and find themselves speaking in front of groups of people, sometimes more than a hundred. They're nervous, flustered, and perspiring – in fact, they're scared, but they STILL DO IT!

That's my favourite kind of speaker because I believe that's where most people are really at – scared!

I ask this question of most of my audiences...

"How many people here have ever been nervous about standing up in public and speaking?"

Most hands are usually raised – and guess what? Look whose hand is also up – mine! I do it for a living but that doesn't stop those butterflies doing loops in my stomach.

As we have already said, according to the 1984 Survey carried out by the New York Times about what people fear most – death comes THIRD. Walking into a room full of strangers comes second and standing up to speak in public tops the list!

So, we would rather leap into a pit of snakes and spiders – or die – than speak in public!

What I would like to do is teach you my 'get out of jail' script. It's the one where somebody says to me "Peter, could you just come to speak for me for a couple of minutes please"

"Fantastic. When?"

"Umm…now."

I'm at the back of the room and I've got to think of something to say!

I haven't got all the answers. I've been speaking for business for a very long time, nearly thirty years, but I've realised that the older I get, the less I know! However, I am going to share with you five tried and tested tips, five tools and five techniques that will help you to develop a reputation for excellence in your field.

FIVE TIPS

TIP 1 – Be In The Moment

"There is in the act of preparing, the ***moment*** *you start caring."*
Winston Churchill

I want you to imagine that it's two in the afternoon, it's a sunny day, I had been out doing some business, and it's been a good morning. I'd had lunch with an old client and the meeting had gone well.

I had my 'shades' on, favourite music playing and was travelling down the motorway at 70mph in the middle lane. I thought, 'Life's great, today's my day and I'm going to enjoy it,' and I made sure the phone was off...

I saw a sign for road works three miles ahead, but the road ahead was clear, so it was going to be great, no delays.

Three miles, two miles, one mile, life's just great. I got to the 800 yards sign, and looked in my rear–view mirror. Big mistake.

Coming up in the outside lane, a car, travelling at about 110 mph, possibly a salesman, probably late for his appointment.

What did I do?

I gripped the steering wheel, hunched my shoulders, looked straight ahead and muttered, "He's not getting past me!" 600 yards, 400 yards and he's still coming... 200 yards, I'm thinking, 'You're never going to get past, I've got you, pal,' and with about 10 yards to go he pulls straight in front of me.

Now what do they do these days with traffic cones and contra flows? They put radar traps on them right at the start, which was exactly where he was, so he stood the car on its nose to get it down to 50mph and Muggins is behind him isn't he!

So I slammed my brakes on, there is tyre smoke everywhere; you could smell the brakes, my heart's beating ten to the dozen.

> Then, I looked in his rear–view mirror and I could see him looking at me as he put his hand up and mouthed, "Thanks."
>
> I thought... well, what would you think?
>
> ...And that was it, we were out of the short road works section in a blink and before I could say or do anything he was off.

Let me ask you a question?

Do you think I was in the moment? Do you think I knew where I was at that moment? Do you think I felt alive?

I believe that it is vitally important that when anyone stands up in front of an audience – even if it's only one person – that you should be in the moment.

BORED, SCARED OR BRILLIANT?

Have you ever been to a presentation where the person speaking obviously didn't want to be there?

Were you bored beyond belief? In this situation, do we listen, do we learn? No.

Generally there are two types of people speaking in business: firstly, those who are just that – bored and disinterested – and I ask why bother being there?

The second type is most other people – i.e. scared!

But just occasionally there is a third, far rarer, animal:

The individual who stands head and shoulders above the rest, perhaps, not someone who is perfect, but someone who clearly knows their craft...

I want you to be one of those few people by the end of this book, so my first suggestion to you is to be in the moment, turn up in mind as well as body!

Think about the last few presentations that you've attended. How would you categorise the speakers? Which of the three categories did they fall into?

Most of us remember the bad ones. We also remember the great ones. Everything in between disappears in the mists of time. So what was the point of spending your time sitting and listening if you didn't get anything from it? You don't want to be guilty of that yourself.

Use every opportunity to not only learn from a speaker's knowledge, but also to learn from their performance. What do they do that works? What do they do that doesn't? Never underestimate the learning you can get from seeing how NOT to do something!

SPEAK FOR YOUR AUDIENCE

To ensure you are in the moment you must be conscious not only of your own presentation, but of the audience and their expectations.

To really be in the moment when you arrive at the place where you will be speaking, you must have done some preparation, and that includes knowing your audience. Ask yourself:

- Who are they?
- What do they already know?
- What are their expectations?
- Who have they heard before?
- Did they like them?

All you have to do is to put yourself in their shoes. If you don't know your audience you can miss the mark by a mile. As soon as you know you have a presentation to do, find out who the audience will be and do some research.

Sometimes it might be as simple as ringing someone up and asking them for a brief. This is certainly true if you're doing a client presentation. There are things that they want to know – but never assume you know what these are, it's safer and easier to ask.

Many people make the mistake of thinking that, if they ask, the client will 'mark them down' for not knowing what they should be doing. I believe that the opposite is true. If there is no clear brief (and sometimes, even if there is) it often wins you lots of 'brownie points' if you take the time to call the client. You don't have to speak to the head honcho, but find someone who you can chat to about what they are trying to achieve, what they've done in the past that they've felt worked, what has changed, what they didn't like – and so on.

How many of your competitors will have bothered? How many of them will be as close to the target as you are? Plus you have an insight into your audience that will make your presentation right on target.

With a bigger audience it's a different challenge. The more people, the more diverse their needs are likely to be. However, if it's a group there is usually some reason for them to come together for this particular event. Why are they a group? What sort of 'carrot' has enticed them to sign up for this event?

If you ask the right questions of the organisers, the person who has asked you to speak, or a few of the people who will be in the audience you'll find it so much easier to be 'on target'.

This will help you to be 'in the moment' because you'll be talking to a specific set of needs and the people with those needs are right there in front of you, so you'll be really focused on them.

To me this is simple – you'll be in the right spirit to serve those who are there.

SPEAK FOR YOURSELF

Speaking for yourself may sound obvious, but many presenters, especially in business, think they are speaking for the company. I'm not suggesting that you ignore the company's viewpoints; if you're representing them you can't do that.

What I am suggesting is that you speak in *your* language, not dry corporate–speak. Use words that people respond to – and you'll get a response!

Have you noticed how frequently people from the corporate world speak about themselves? They are always saying, "We have done this...", "We believe that...", "Our research says that..." And the audience is thinking "What's this got to do with me?" and "When is it time for coffee?"

Don't fall into this tired, third person approach. Use statements that talk about the audience – use *you* and *your*, not *We, Us*, or *Our*. You'll keep your audience awake and you'll help yourself to feel in the moment, not reciting some boring message that obviously doesn't excite you.

ENERGISE BEFORE OPENING

If you find yourself feeling either tired or nervous you won't make the impression that you should to get and keep the audience's attention. Nerves can make you yawn too – as you tend to take shallow breaths and get less oxygen.

To really make an impact you need to be energised – and to look it. There are things that will help you to feel energised, try them and find something that works for you:

1. Smile – it releases endorphins that make you feel better.
2. Take deep breaths and swing your arms around for a minute – this will get the blood oxygenised and rushing about with more enthusiasm.
3. Visualise yourself walking onto the platform full of energy and enthusiasm, do this several times and it will start to establish your subconscious 'matching' system. This encourages you to take the actions that match the 'reality' that you've created.
4. If all else fails, find somewhere away from everyone and jump up and down shouting "I FEEL FANTASTIC!" This will not only make you feel better, it will probably make you laugh. Be warned that it could have serious consequences if anyone else sees you doing this – they may think you've lost it altogether and send for the straight–jacket!

I can guarantee you'll be in the moment if you feel energised.

So that's the first tip: Don't be bored, don't be scared; speak for your audience, speak for yourself and energise before opening – *be in the moment.*

And remember to be in a spirit to serve!

TIP 2 – Be Yourself

*"Be a first rate version of **yourself**, not a second rate version of someone else."*
Judy Garland

We've already discussed the issue of using a speaking style that relates to your audience. However, there's more to 'being yourself' than simply using your own normal language.

The top speakers have strong personalities that come shining through when they're on the platform. They're not trying to be anyone else – the audience have come to listen to them because of who they are, as well as for what they have to say.

Think of the people that you have seen speak that have really made an impression. I bet that you almost felt you 'knew' them by the end of the speech.

Think about the world's renowned speakers – Tom Peters, Jay Abrahams, Warren Buffett – they are remembered not only because they have a powerful message, but because they have such a strong personality that they put it over in a totally memorable way.

What about all the politicians? You remember the ones that really seem to be 'themselves' rather than a mouthpiece for their party.

So you need to be yourself when you speak to make your message memorable.

LEAVE YOUR TITLE AT YOUR DESK

Many people find it hard to forget their title when they speak. They walk into their presentation as a job function.

It's surprising how much of what is going on in your head will influence not only your actions, but other people's responses too. If you are thinking "I've got to make this presentation because I'm the sales manager and it's my job to get this information over to them," your audience will be thinking, "It's only the sales manager with some information that's probably boring."

What sort of presentation do you think that will turn out to be?

When you're talking to friends about something that you are passionate about, how do you talk? Try and use those skills to get your message across in business too.

People don't want 'the sales manager's presentation'; they want 'Bob's ideas'. They don't want the corporate message; they want the boss to talk to them personally – so the boss has to be a person they can relate to.

So don't walk into your presentation as 'The Sales Manager' or 'The Managing Director' or 'The Business Owner' – be *you* and you'll come over much more naturally.

WHAT MAKES YOU YOU?

That may sound ridiculous, but most of us have no idea what makes people warm to us and what our special skills are. So how do you find this out? Simple – you ask.

Ask those people closest to you what they think you are good at. Ask them what they like about you (and, if you're brave, what they dislike).

Think about what people have said about you in the past – what sort of feedback do you get regularly?

Frances was the life and soul of the party – actually, everyone except her mother called her Frankie. She was always fooling around and was constantly surrounded by laughter. She was known for making people laugh because of her ability to recount everyday situations in a ridiculous fashion.

One day, a well–meaning friend said to her, "You are so funny, you should do stand–up." There was a local comedy club that had a 'showcase' spot and, before Frankie realised it, she'd signed up for a showcase for three weeks time.

She had an attack of terror, then decided to do it anyway and started collecting her material for an act. She gathered all the jokes she knew and then started picking the brains of all her friends. She put the jokes together in groups that related and practised whilst driving about in her car, in the shower, and anywhere else she got a few quiet moments.

The day arrived and she turned up with her friends. At last it was the showcase – the MC announced her and, with shaking knees, she got up and delivered her showcase.

Her friends valiantly supported her, but hardly anyone else laughed. It was the longest three minutes of her life and at the end she got a very lukewarm reception.

"At least nobody really heckled," said one of her friends. Frankie just wanted to get out of there – and probably had one or two more drinks than was sensible to drown her sorrows.

She never attempted stand–up again, but her friends still think she is the funniest person they know.

So what happened?

Frankie's strength was telling stories – making the mundane seem ridiculous, exaggerating the facts and making people larger than life. That isn't what she attempted to do at the comedy club – she tried to tell jokes.

She was way outside her comfort zone and it just wasn't her thing. She wasn't being herself – and the audience didn't warm to her.

There's no reason why she shouldn't have told stories, but her perception of what was needed was jokes. She didn't feel that telling stories was 'funny'.

When you next know you're going to make a presentation make sure you don't fall into the same track as Frankie – do it your way.

It will bring your presentation to life and you'll get a much warmer response from your audience.

PEOPLE BUY PEOPLE

Your audience will 'buy' you first and only listen to your message if you've sold yourself well. It's called building rapport. When you're making a presentation you need to try and do that as quickly as possible – in the first minute or two.

When you start to speak you must be speaking *to* the audience – not *at* them. One of the easiest ways to include your audience is to ask them a question – even if you don't really want them to answer it. They'll all start answering it in their heads and it will get them thinking about what you're saying.

Let's give it a try:

"What would you do if you found that your very expensive car had just been crashed by your best friend?"

Now what's going on in your head? Are you imagining what you would be thinking, what you would be feeling? That's what happens when you ask your audience a question.

Of course, you have to make sure it's the right question! Make it relevant and thought provoking – and in relation to what you are talking about. For example

"Would you like me to tell you a story that would guarantee to help you to understand your wife or husband?"

This could be a great opener for someone speaking to an audience where it was full of people that had challenges with their partners etc.

People will quickly feel that you've 'included' them and warm to you. You're well on the way to building a great rapport with your audience.

So that's the second tip: leave your title at your desk, don't speak as a 'position' but as a 'person'; be natural and use your natural style, don't try to copy someone else; and build rapport with your audience, get them to feel part of the presentation. Just *be yourself*.

TIP 3 – Understand Your Purpose

"He was wont to ***speak*** *plain and to the* ***purpose****,*
like an honest man and a soldier."
William Shakespeare

This is may appear obvious – and we'll be discussing this in depth later, but when someone asks you to speak you need to know why.

There are many versions of 'why' – but most of us tend to think 'why me?'

However, much more important is to be clear about what is expected of you. There are a number of reasons that people make presentations:

Once you are clear about the reason you'll be making this presentation you'll find it much easier to focus on achieving your object.

THE INFORMATION PRESENTATION

This is where you are the means of presenting a new project, a change in strategy, launching the latest product or service your company has devised or addressing any audience that doesn't know what you are about to tell them.

Think of this as being a 'talking newspaper'. These sorts of presentation can be dry and boring – but that's not how a newspaper works! Grab them with a headline, make your first paragraph a hook to keep them listening. Give them facts and figures and anecdotal evidence too (remember, People buy People).

Work on your presentation from a newspaper point of view and you'll be well on the way to success.

TO EDUCATE YOUR AUDIENCE

Arguably, this might also be classified as an 'information presentation', however, it's more than that. You're not only passing on information, you're helping people to learn – so what do you have to do to help them remember what you're saying?

There are some scary statistics that tell us that people only remember a small part of what we say.

A speaker normally says only 80% of what he/she planned to say. Only 60% of this is heard by the audience.

- After three hours only 40% is remembered
- After three days only 15% is remembered
- After three months 5% or less is remembered

You might wonder why we bother! However, the more involvement you get, the more that figure improves.

Visual aids – as long as they are visual AIDS, not your presentation notes on PowerPoint slides – work very well. People relate well to pictures, charts, diagrams, etc.

With visual input the figures are:

- After three days 60% is remembered
- After three months 40–50% is remembered

That's not all – if you provide handouts or notes that figure improves further, especially if you have managed to get your audience to write on them. This means that:

- After three days 80% is remembered
- After three months 60–70% is remembered

So you know what you need to do if your presentation is aimed at education.

THE 'TURN'

Sometimes the role of the presenter is simply to entertain. This is less common in business, but not nearly as rare as you might think.

Now and then there will be a delegation that nobody knows what to do with for a half hour between meetings. An unsuspecting member of one of the management teams is usually dragged in to 'give them an idea of what your lot do' – make it interesting, keep it light.

The secret of entertaining talks is to tell stories. Now, that means putting the human beings in the front line! Don't talk about the systems and numbers, talk about Jenny and George and Shahin.

Use the people to explain how the department operates; tell anecdotes about how something came about. This is the key to making it interesting – or entertaining.

Here's an example from my friend Lesley, whose team this really was:

> When we started out there were just four of us. Karim, who looks after the orders side of things. He's fairly quiet, very conscientious and lives in a paper mountain, but he seems to be able to keep it all moving! He always knows exactly what we have on order and is great at dealing with the suppliers' accounts departments; they know that the documentation will be perfect every time. There's Bernadette, more often known as Berna, petite and pretty, who is just amazing at keeping all the administration in order – she always knows where we're up to with everything. I suppose she's our office 'memory'! Then there's Aaron – he's the one that goes and meets suppliers and organises the deliveries.
>
> He can always get things done when everyone says it's impossible. I don't think it's anything to do with the fact that he is tall, handsome and charming, but I guess it helps! I took on the management of the team a couple of years back and we've really moved on with a bigger team and also more responsibilities.
>
> We've expanded to eight people now – there's Ingrid who looks after the numbers side, there's such a lot to record with stocks in and out, and she not only keeps track of materials for production, but also for all our consumables. Ingrid can be a bit moody, but she definitely gets results. Now she has Alicia and Hannah helping out things are much better. These two couldn't be more different, Alicia is quiet and barely utters a word, whilst Hannah is eager, extrovert and, sometimes, volatile.

Ingrid and Hannah have had their collisions, but Ingrid is very good with the computer and has come up with lots of time saving strategies that have made a real difference to our turnaround time, so she just needs a bit of managing.

Ingrid is the reason that our supplier accounts now go through the accounting approval process in just two days instead of five. She's a great negotiator and managed to sell her ideas to our accounts team – and believe me, that's a real achievement!

Mel joined us to deal with new suppliers and she has a constant stream of applications to deal with. She's great fun and always ready to laugh, but very organised, so I just get the final lists to deal with, which makes my life much easier.

Given that we get over 50 applications a month from suppliers, she's kept busy looking after these – and she helps Berna some of the time too.

We've been working on a multi–skilling programme over the past few months to ensure that every one of us has cover so we can go on holiday – or be ill!

We started out as a group of four individuals – but I'm proud to say we are now a team that works very well together.

Lesley's story is full of people and helps you to really 'see' them all, and their situation.

The people bring the process to life – you would add more detail into your story to demonstrate the key things you wanted to get over, but the people make it human and much easier to listen to.

TO CONVINCE SOMEONE

This is a tougher job than most. When you've been cast in the role of advocate – think lawyer. What does a lawyer do to make their case?

That's simple! It's all based on evidence. This means that you need to have all the evidence available to make your case.

Do your research, get all the data and statistics together, talk to people who have experience or knowledge that will help your argument. Then learn how to ask good questions – the ones to which there is only one answer!

Questions like:

Are you interested in increasing our profits by 20%?

Would you like to see our company topping
our industry for production?

If the sales increased by 12% this year,
would that be good for us?

Nobody in any company could say 'no' to any of these!

Put your case together so that you have the evidence followed by the conclusion and then the 64 dollar question. If you assemble all this properly there will only be one possible answer.

However, do be warned that, if you are good at this, you will almost certainly be asked to do this again – and again!

TO GET A DECISION

Many presentations are actually sales pitches. They are purely to get a group of people to decide on which option they like best. Advertising agencies do presentations, new suppliers do presentations, law and accountancy firms do presentations; they're all trying to get a decision.

Getting a decision is based on understanding what is wanted. This means that your presentation must hit the target accurately. More research is needed.

- Find out what they already have
- Find out what they've liked in the past
- Find out what they said they wanted
- If in doubt, call them and ask for more details

Then follow the classic sales formula:

Sell yourself. We've already talked about building rapport. Make them feel that you are easy to talk to and someone who it will be good to work with. Smiles and open gestures, not frowns and arms folded!

Sell your experience and your company's track record. Give a rundown of your own background/experience (briefly) so they can be confident that you know what you're talking about. Also give a few credentials for the organisation – current biggest clients, successful projects, and so on.

Outline all the key things they said they wanted. There is usually a brief to work to for most pitches – make sure you have all the details of what that brief said covered. As we said above – if you aren't sure ask!

Explain how your proposal meets each of those key things. This is the key part of the exercise where you say, "You wanted X and you'll get X when we deliver Y and Z." You need to do this for each point.

Finally you ask them for the decision – and this is the point when you say no more! If your presentation doesn't finish here then your career may do! Once you've wrapped it up, you don't say any more until they've given their decision. If you carry on talking you can talk yourself, and your company, out of the running.

So that's tip number three: *Understand your purpose* – know whether your presentation is to inform, educate, entertain, convince or to get a decision.

TIP 4 – Be Results Focused

*"It's time to take action – to put into practice a new approach that **focuses** on **results** and measurable improvements."*
Bob Riley

You can be a great talker but still not get a result. Let me give you an example of how people misunderstand what a presentation is all about.

A friend of mine, Lesley Morrissey used to live in Dubai. She was conducting a training course in presentation skills for a group of trainees, mostly Arabic men, but fluent in English. However, there were three Arabic girls, all wearing the flowing gowns that Arabic ladies wear, but only one, Maha, had covered her face.

For the final day Lesley had asked them to prepare a ten minute presentation on a subject of their own choice. A number of the men were quite happy with that and were fairly blasé about the whole thing. All the girls were nervous and went off to do their preparation.

On the day everyone got their opportunity to present – and to be filmed. It was quickly apparent who had done their 'homework', and who hadn't. Khalil offered to go first and talked for 10 minutes about... well, that was the problem, nobody was really sure. He definitely talked for ten minutes, he said a lot, but when he got to the end everyone was wondering what that was all about.

Then Fatima did her presentation. She was a bit nervous, and had chosen a subject with which she was unfamiliar. She had worked hard to gather the information together, but it soon became clear that she didn't really know her subject well as she got tangled up in the detail. At the end she had given a lot of information, but hadn't made any particular point.

Some more of the men presented with varying results and Maha then took to the floor – she was very nervous and had a big drawback to overcome, nobody could see her face, only her eyes. However, she had worked hard to create some visuals and did a great presentation that went from point to point and came to a conclusion at the end.

Saeed then got up and did a demonstration of how you check your blood sugar if you're a diabetic. He explained what diabetes was and the different forms it could take and then went through the process that you have to follow to check your blood sugar and what you do after that to ensure you don't go into a coma. It was interesting; it had been worked out; and there was a beginning, a middle and an end. Everyone understood what it was about, there was a clear outcome – they all knew the basics about diabetes and how to carry out the process Saeed had described.

So who did it right and who needed to go back to the drawing board and work at it?

ANYONE CAN TALK

You need to be clear about not only your path, but also your destination, when you make a presentation.

We can all talk – we do it all the time, but only those that have been well–trained are good at talking to a point. Just think how conversations you have with colleagues and friends go all over the place. You ramble and waffle – I know I do! Things come up that distract your attention and off you go in a different direction.

Have you ever left a session with a couple of friends and then suddenly remember something you were going to say, but never did, because the conversation went off on a new route? We've all done it. The moment has gone and things move on, then it's too late.

That's fine in conversation – but it's lethal when you're presenting. You can't afford to ramble, because your audience won't always follow your thought processes when you do. You need to be absolutely clear on where you're going – or you'll get lost! Don't do what Khalil did.

KNOW YOUR STUFF

Make sure you're working on a subject you know well, know where you want to go and the steps that will get you there.

Never follow Fatima's example. If anyone ever tries to persuade you to make a presentation on a subject you don't know well, refuse. Suggest someone else, but don't give in. It may be attractive to be in the limelight, but if you fall flat on your face because your lack of knowledge trips you up, it's not a pleasant place to be at all.

Lots of people think they can 'get away with it' – but it really isn't worth it. Someone will see through you, and people talk. As soon as it is known that you are inaccurate in one thing it brings everything you say into question.

This is another good reason for making sure you do your research.

If you understand your subject thoroughly you'll be able to talk about it with confidence and authority. Your presentation will have a better chance of staying on course and arriving at the destination you have chosen. Remember Maha and Saeed? At the end of their presentation nobody was in any doubt that they knew what they were talking about, they had made it clear for the audience to understand.

You may know your stuff but don't *wing it*!

I was asked to speak for a well–known bank at their New Year launch as a keynote speaker to help them get their new and punchy message out to the business market.

It went very well and I was asked to stay on and listen to the end of the conference which was to be closed by the head of the bank in a rousing 'let's get to it' finale.

The individual came on to rapturous applause.

He told the standard corporate joke to great laughter.

He over–ran by fifteen minutes to no complaint.

And he finished to thunderous applause – a job well done.

After exiting the stage the individual came over to me and said, "Well? How did I do?"

In these situations I always say, "Well done!" with sincerity as I admire and respect anyone who has the courage to face an audience.

"No, really," he said, "I want your professional opinion."

Now, being honest as I am, anyone who ever asks me what I think gets the truth. I'm the kind of guy who calls a spade a shovel.

"OK – can I ask you a question?" I asked

"Shoot!" he drawled.

"How long had you practised the speech?"

The presenter replied (looking away from me), "Oh, I had mulled it over for several weeks and got the bones together a few days ago."

I remained silent and kept looking at him.

After an eternity he looked directly at me and cracked. "All right, to be truthful, in the car on the way over from the airport – about half an hour beforehand – there has been so much pressure lately. How did you know?"

I looked at him and said, "Because I was you.

I used to have a major team of people working for me in corporate land with large financial implications and I used to revel in coming to a conference such as this to see if I could pull it off. I had people speak to me afterwards who would say they didn't know how I did it.

Well, they would do – wouldn't they! I was the boss.

The question was – how crazy can you get?

How much respect did I ultimately give them?

Was I focused on them or myself?"

He went very quiet and said it was sobering food for thought.

It's not just about knowing what you want – it's about what your audience needs!

We both knew that if you wing it you are doing your audience a disservice. If you take on the responsibility of delivering information, it must be the best that you can do, not just what you can be bothered to do.

KNOW WHAT YOU WANT

Before you begin to plan your presentation know what you want people to know when you've finished – even if it's a small result, that doesn't matter. What matters is that you have a plan that has an outcome – what do you want people to do as a result of your presentation?

This is easy if the answer is 'to make a decision', but sometimes the outcome isn't a crystal clear as that.

An outcome could be:

- To make your audience feel more positive and empowered
- To sign up to a project
- To support you when you put yourself up for election
- To do something that will improve their lives
- To join your team
- To agree on a decision

Or many other things. As long as you know where you are going and what you want to achieve, your audience will follow your lead.

So that's tip number four: *Be results focused* – don't just talk, make sure you know your subject well and be clear about what you want people to do when you've finished.

TIP 5 – Be A Giver

*"The heart of the **giver** makes the gift dear and precious."*
Martin Luther King JN

Some presenters give, some don't. What do I mean by 'give'? Well, I mean that you should be sharing your knowledge rather than preaching or lecturing. Let me explain:

- Don't tell people what to do, show them how to do it.
- Don't tell them what is right, help them to understand *why* it is right
- Don't give them instructions, give them guidance, advice and support.

INCLUDE THEM IN

Give your expertise, knowledge and experience in a way that gives value to your audience. Make them feel part of the presentation not a separate entity; there only to listen.

Give them permission to get involved to take what's on offer, to make it work for them.

PRESENT AND STAY ...

Don't be a 'turn up, present and leave' person – get there early, meet people and then stay around to talk to those who were too nervous to put their hand up and ask questions. Give your time to them, not only on the 'platform', but off it as well.

Being a giver may mean you'll also become a receiver. They say 'what goes around, comes around' – that's been proven over and over. You give to people and someone, somewhere, will give to you. It may not be any of the people that you've given to over the years, but it does come back to you somehow.

However, for me I just give anyway. My philosophy is simple – to give is to receive. By seeing the light go on in just one person's eyes in an audience is enough for me – I've done my job that day.

Many professional speakers find that this is the time when they meet the people who will be their next clients. If they just left at the end of the speech they'd lose a lot of opportunities!

So that's tip number five: *Be a giver* – share your time, knowledge and experience and include the audience in your presentation.

FIVE TOOLS

TOOL 1 – Why?

"Sometimes when I'm talking, my words can't keep up with my thoughts. I wonder ***why*** *we think faster than we* ***speak****. Probably so we can think twice."*
Bill Watterson

Have you ever been in a situation where your boss has come up to you and asked you to make a presentation, but you never knew why? Were you on the verge of panicking? Did words appear in your head that aren't repeatable? It's certainly happened to me on occasions.

Why stand up and speak?

My simple suggestion to you is this – if someone asks you to stand up and speak on any subject from 30 seconds to a couple of hours, ask yourself the question 'Why?' Or perhaps if you're employed, ask the person asking you to speak, 'Why?'

Here is my advice: if you can't answer the question 'Why?' whatever you do, don't agree to speak! Just don't do it!

If *you* don't know why you're standing up to speak in the first place, is it fair to say that the audience probably won't understand why you're talking to them either? Because if you don't know, you can be sure that they won't know!

People sometimes say to me, "Oh, you mean the point of the speech?"

No, it's nothing to do with the point of the speech... this is about you as an individual. What is driving you to stand up?

The six serving men of Rudyard Kipling – who, what, when, where, why, and how – are very useful words, and why is the most powerful.

Ask yourself the following questions:

- What's in it for the audience?
- What's in it for you?

- What are the benefits to the audience to listen to you?
- Understand why you have been asked to speak
- Understand why they chose you

Think about the answers to these questions.

WHAT'S IN IT FOR THE AUDIENCE?

Yes, there is the issue of purpose, we've already talked about that – in relation to the presentation itself – but what can *you* add to this presentation?

The secret is to know what *you* offer the audience. What will they get if you make this presentation that they wouldn't get from anyone else?

Once you're clear about that you should be able to answer the second question.

WHAT'S IN IT FOR YOU?

What will you gain from making the presentation? If the answer is 'nothing', then don't do it. Say "thank you for asking" and suggest someone else who would be suitable.

If your job depends on it, then you might want to ask the person making the request what the benefits for your career progression will be.

Having said this, there is usually something for you in any presentation you make. We all learn from doing things, we learn what works and what doesn't. We learn how to present information in a way that engages our audiences and we hone our skills as speakers, so don't just write off a presentation as being 'of no use at all'. If you want to get something from it, you'll find something of value to you.

WHAT ARE THE BENEFITS TO THE AUDIENCE TO LISTEN TO YOU?

Think about what your knowledge will give the audience. Be specific! What benefits can you offer them that they won't get any other way? This is an extension of the first question, but you really need to pin down the detail here.

Imagine you're sitting in the audience yourself. What would make you feel that sitting still for this presentation had been really worth it?

This might include specific facts that you can give them; it might be the ability to explain a particularly complex concept in simple language; it might be that you can tell a story that will help them to remember critical information better; it might be – well, you know your own skills – what else might they get from listening to you?

UNDERSTAND WHY YOU HAVE BEEN ASKED TO SPEAK

If you've asked the person who has suggested that you should make this presentation, you may have already got the answer to this. Although it may not be all of the answer!

There are many reasons why people are asked to make presentations.

- It could be that you have a particularly good voice to listen to (although that alone is not a good enough reason for you to agree to make a presentation).
- It may be that you have a particular bank of knowledge that will ensure that the audience get more from the presentation than if someone less knowledgeable were to make it (that's a good reason).
- It might be because you have a particular role or status in your organisation that will lend credibility to the message (this might be a good reason if you have the relevant knowledge as well).

- It might be because you are someone that people respect and listen to (again, not a good enough reason on its own, but alongside sufficient knowledge, could be added value).
- It may be because someone feels that if you are not asked you will be upset or angry.

I'm sure you can come up with lots more reasons why people are asked to make presentations – not all of them valid.

The question is do *you* think that the reason for you being asked to speak is a good one? Can you see why you would be a good choice for this presentation?

If you can't, maybe you need to ask some more questions.

UNDERSTAND WHY YOU!

This may seem to be the same question as the last one – but it isn't! Understanding why someone else has asked you to speak is only half of it. You need to understand that they are right.

Once you've found out the reason behind the request, can you accept that the reason is a good one? Does it make sense to you that you should make this presentation?

If you still don't see that you are the right person to make this presentation then you really ought to say "No."

If you have doubts, your audience will quickly sense that and it will devalue your presentation. Better not to make a presentation than to make a poor one.

> I said in the introduction to the book that my favourite speaker is typically a charity co–ordinator, who works with their charity as a volunteer because they're passionate about the cause. They probably also have a day job.
>
> The end to this story is that, after they have been scared to death facing their number one fear, they sit back down next to someone who will always say, "Thanks for taking the time to come and see us – I don't know how you speak in front of all these people I'm sure I could never do it."

...and then they hear the magic words,

"But it's clear to me you are passionate about the charity and care for the people it serves."

You see it doesn't matter how technically good you are – it's all about why you're speaking. The audience will support and respect you if it's clear you believe in what you're saying and you have their interests at heart...

FIVE SIMPLE TIPS TO HELP YOU UNDERSTAND 'WHY YOU?'

1. Don't skimp on this part of the process – take the time you need.
2. When you understand, ask others to say what they think but be careful whom you choose.
3. Recognise your passions are not always as strong in others. Accept where people are at.
4. If you use emotive words to describe your 'why' – live them. You can only be passionate, or not. You can't be 'quite passionate'.
5. Don't underestimate yourself. If you believe it's worth speaking about, it probably is!

So Tool Number One is to *understand why you're being asked to speak and why you're the right person to speak.*

TOOL 2 – Point!

*"When you have an important **point** to make, don't try to be subtle or clever. Use a pile driver. Hit the **point** once. Then come back and hit it again. Then hit it a third time – a tremendous whack."*
Winston Churchill

What's the point of your speech?

Have you ever listened to somebody and thought they were great? Perhaps they were funny, entertaining even. Yet when you are asked what the point of the speech was, you couldn't put your finger on it? Are you sure there was one?

If you've ever experienced that you know that you must decide the point of your speech. Before you get started you need to have a clear idea of where your presentation is going. A very powerful phrase is one coined originally by Stephen Covey and is 'Start with the end in mind'.

- Understand the key message first
- Split the key message into the relevant parts of its make up
- Make one key point per part
- List them together and see if they make sense
- If not go back to the first item in this list!

Let's look at these in more detail:

UNDERSTAND THE KEY MESSAGE FIRST

This will make the rest of your presentation planning relatively easy. Now think about this – if you could only tell your audience one critical piece of information, what would it be?

Once you've got that clear in your mind you will have identified your key message.

Most speakers have a number of points to make, but the good ones are all contributing to one main message. What is yours?

I always liken this to a favourite trip or holiday.

Sometime I will ask my audience – has anyone flown to Disneyland recently?

Nearly always someone has in the last twelve months

I ask them some questions:

What airline? What flight number? Which airport? And so on.

Then I ask this question:

"Once you were through security and they have called your flight; if you had walked up to the plane and no one was there and the plane had no visible sign of where it was going – would you get on it?"

Everyone always says "No!"

So my question to you is simple why would you start a speech if you didn't know its destination?

Yet so many people see the end as a means to sit down whereas the truth is that the end is the most important part. It's when you arrive at Disneyland for the audience – it's the bit they actually remember if you let them!

So "Start with the end in mind!"

SPLIT THE KEY MESSAGE INTO THE RELEVANT PARTS

Once you have your key message clear in your head, you will need to split it up into sections. Not too many, but all must be focused on getting that key message across.

The two most obvious examples of this are:

- Tell them what you're going to tell them
- Tell them
- Tell them what you told them

This is particularly good for informational type presentations. An alternative approach is:

- Address a current problem
- Explain the pain associated with that problem
- Suggest the best solution
- Confirm the result

This is a better approach for a persuasive/sales approach.

MAKE ONE KEY POINT PER PART

Now you have your 'skeleton plan' you need to put some flesh on the bones. What will be the *point* of each of the parts you have created? Each must stand alone, whilst at the same time contributing to the main key message.

So if you've chosen a persuasive approach you now need to establish what current problem needs to change and why. Describe it, explain the pain.

Now you need to tell them what is going on now, and what steps are being taken to change the situation that used to exist. Usually what's happening now is not the end of the journey – but there must be some real, and interesting, detail about how things are moving on and getting better. Or, at the very least, firm plans are in place for this to happen.

The last section is where you describe what the future will be like, what benefits people will experience and how things will generally be better. It's your opportunity to really create a strong vision for your audience – they can check out the past, they can see what's going on now – but the future is where you really are their only means of 'seeing' it.

You'll have lots of bits of information that will add to each of these parts that will reinforce each point. Just make sure that they all lead to your main point at the end.

LIST THEM TOGETHER AND SEE IF THEY MAKE SENSE

It's a good move to create a 'map' of your journey from beginning to end so you can see how these points fit together. After all, you wouldn't try and explain a complicated route to someone without having it clear in your own mind first.

There should be some flow to the 'map' and a clear step by step process that makes it easy for people to follow. Don't over–estimate people's ability to see where you're going – you really must give them a clear picture and lots of signposts along the way.

At the same time it's really important that the progression is logical. Each piece of information needs to be relevant, both to the point that it supports and to the main point.

For instance, if you're talking about cars and their effect on the environment – you need to have a clear structure and to tell people that you are going to look at the development of the internal combustion engine, the volume of traffic today and how the emission levels are having an impact. You don't want to wander off into the differences between cars, lorries, motorbikes, what happens on and around racing circuits and other miscellaneous bits of information. You don't want to confuse people, after all.

Don't *wing it*!

> I was asked to speak at a well known business school for a group of past students and to share with them simple techniques on speaking and presenting. We all had a great time, as they were an enthusiastic bunch willing to learn.
>
> After my presentation there was a short break, which was followed by a respected member of the Faculty giving his views of where the school was developing in the coming years.
>
> The individual came to the front of the stage and ceremonially threw away the CD of his PowerPoint presentation and said, "Having listened to Peter, I don't need this!"
>
> My instant thought was – I hope he knows his stuff!

Unfortunately, he didn't and had a terrible time for the next forty minutes or so.

Afterwards we had a chat. He said it had been the worst forty minutes of his life. He couldn't understand why a presentation he had given so many times had suddenly become an issue.

I explained that it could happen to anyone. I explained that the unfortunate side–effect of a PowerPoint presentation is the lack of connection to it by the majority of presenters.

Most use it as a map to stay on track, which meant that as soon as he threw it away he was lost – literally! And, of course, so was the audience!

This is just one of the reasons why four out of five presentations fail.

He resolved to use PowerPoint as an aid only, for effect, not as a map. I'm pleased to say that he has since become a good speaker without needing PowerPoint as a prop!

You can add facts, statistics, data, charts, stories and anecdotes – but they must all earn their place in your presentation. If they're not working towards your main point – be ruthless!

IF NOT, GO BACK TO THE FIRST ITEM IN THIS LIST!

If the sub–headings you've created don't produce a logical progression to your main message, then you need to revisit item one! Understand your key message.

If your sub–points don't seem to fit in with it you have one of two choices:

- Change the main point
- Change or delete the supporting point in question

Most of the time the answer is the latter of these two. After all the main point IS the main point! If you haven't created a plan that takes you to that point, you have gone off track and need to review your journey.

Try again and resist the urge to put sub–points in that don't support your main message. These points may be important – but not to this particular presentation.

FIVE SIMPLE TIPS TO HELP YOU GET YOUR POINT ACROSS

1. When making a one, five, or ten–minute speech you can probably only fit one point in.
2. If you are making a forty–five minute speech, three to five points are the maximum, but go for three or less if possible!
3. Remember a great phrase – 'Less is more!'
4. Decide your point before you stand up and speak, and stick to it.
5. Understand that not everyone may agree with you!

Tool Number Two is simply to *be clear about the whole point of your presentation.*

TOOL 3 – Close

*"There must be a beginning of any great matter, but the continuing unto the end until it be thoroughly **finished** yields the true glory."*
Francis Drake

We've reached the third step. Most people, when they start a speech, start at the beginning. Please don't do that!

Again I would remind you – start with the end in mind!

Whilst it may seem logical to work from the beginning to the end, if you know where you're ending you'll find the beginning and the middle so much easier.

Remember our friend, the charity co–ordinator? If that was you I can guarantee you'd know why you were standing up to speak.

- You're supporting a specific charity and it's important to you.
- It makes a difference for whatever your personal reasons are and you're going to be there on a Tuesday night to collect the cheque and give a few words.

You know your *Why*.

You know your *Point* – in this particular case to thank the people who have collected the money by being interested in what they did.

That's the point, to thank the people who did it, for the way they did it (quiz night, jumble sale, sponsored walk, or whatever they've done to raise the cash) and that they did it!

The next thing you need to do is ask yourself, "How do I finish the speech?"

The Close is the finish of the speech.

You must make your point in the Close – decide what you want to say and then practise it. It's really important that this key message comes over loud and clear.

If that's to say, "Your money will save the lives of twenty children, and I know they'd want me to thank you." Then this is where you say it.

Make sure the Close is strong, it signals that it's the end and you know it word–perfect.

Then time it. Know how long the lead up and final point take so you can be sure that this part of your presentation won't make you run over your time allowed.

- Practise saying why you're speaking and say thank you.
- Saying thank you gives two results – it's polite and it tells the audience you've finished!
- Use the rhythm of threes see page 154.
- Look in the mirror and see if your close gives you the effect you want.
- Practise this more than any other area.
- Give yourself a time limit.

PRACTISE SAYING WHY YOU'RE SPEAKING AND SAY THANK YOU

Try your close out to see if it makes sense and if it does, well done, you know how to close instinctively. However, most of us have to work at this. Just stating your point sometimes comes over as a bit abrupt.

What words can you use to lead up to your close? How can you signal to the audience that the end is in sight?

Some people like to make their point and finish simply with 'thank you', others like to lead up to their close with "I'd like to thank you for spending this time with me today. Before I finish I'd just like to say..." followed by your key message.

There are many ways to do this. Try different closes and find one that you feel comfortable with.

I use several finishes. The two I'm most well known for are;

"And remember... If I can help you in any way, just let me know!"

"I want you to feel free to speak and be a natural presenter!"

However sometimes the best finishes are those that are truly inspired – but be careful!

I was speaking in front of 150 students in a plenary session at a University as the invited keynote speaker. The audience was fantastic – full of youthful enthusiasm and desire to learn.

After I had finished there were some more formalities and I was thanked again and invited to say goodbye – something I wasn't expecting.

I thought to myself what on earth am I going to say?

There was a hushed silence and I said a quick prayer (although I am not a religious person).

I simply said to myself please give me something that can make a difference for these people... and then it came to me.

I remembered an event in my life when I was the same age as the audience some thirty years before – something that made a profound difference to me at that time yet I hadn't mentioned this even to my family or anyone else before.

The ending went something like this...

"Looking at you now reminds me of when, at about your age, I went on my first holiday abroad – to Bulgaria. OK so it was cheap at the time!

"I met a man from Bristol called John and immediately liked him – and it was one of those times when you would like to spend more time with someone, but the plane times just didn't match – and he was off the next day.

"John was taking the holiday that he and his wife had saved for over a very long time. Unfortunately, she had passed away with cancer before the holiday, but she had made John promise he would still go anyway – which he reluctantly did.

"The last time I saw John was in a lift at the top of a multi story hotel complex as we realized we would not meet again he looked me straight in the eyes as the lift doors closed and said – 'Have a Great Life.'

...And so I say to you all here today as a simple messenger 'Have A Great Life!'

Thank You."

It got a two–minute standing ovation and the audience touched me in a way they will never know.

A speaker pal of mine – the Minister for Inspiration, Richard Wilkins, when asked "How is life treating you today Richard?" always answers, "Life is treating me as well as I'm treating it!"

On this day life certainly treated me exceptionally well.

USE THE RHYTHM OF THREES

The rhythm of threes can be very powerful and is easy to think through. Examples are the easiest way to understand the concept:

"Ladies and gentleman, it's been a pleasure to be with you, a pleasure to share my ideas and it will be a pleasure to see you again soon."

Or, if you've chosen a particular approach (as we outlined earlier) you might choose to say something like, "You've heard about our past, you've contributed to our present and we hope you'll be part of our future."

Threes have a strong memory factor – they help your audience to remember something better, even if they don't remember the actual words.

Plan what you want to say and see if you can find three things that sit together to help you use the strength of the rhythm of threes.

LOOK IN THE MIRROR AND SEE IF YOUR CLOSE GIVES YOU THE EFFECT YOU WANT

When you finish speaking are you smiling, concerned, happy, or sad? Do you look the way you want the audience to be?

Did you know that the audience will often reflect your emotions? If you can use your own emotions to influence theirs you'll be doing a great job.

If you don't feel emotions then you shouldn't be doing this presentation. Good presenters have passion. If you don't have passion for your subject, find someone else to do it – who has the passion!

If you have strong emotions, it will add depth and colour to your presentation – and this is most important at the end. It's where you have to really mean what you say to help the audience to remember your message.

Be careful that the emotion you are demonstrating isn't relief that it's over!

PRACTISE THIS MORE THAN ANY OTHER AREA!

This part of your presentation is the bit that your audience should remember best. It needs to be word perfect, strong, and to convey your message clearly.

- If it's a call to action then make sure that is clear.
- If it's a thank you for something that the audience has done, make sure it is sincere.
- If it's information that they need to know, ensure it has been clearly summarized and the application for the information is spelled out for them.

There's nothing worse than a presentation that stumbles to a halt, or just peters out. All that effort you've put into developing it just disappears like smoke in the breeze.

People might remember your ending – because they were surprised that it was the end – that's not what you're standing up for!

Choose your words, practise it over and over until it rings true and clear.

GIVE YOURSELF A TIME LIMIT

Your close can include a summary of what you've said, "In brief, we've explored..."

- It can be the conclusion of your presentation "As a result of all this it's clear that..."
- It can be a few crucial facts "So next time you see X happening, remember that..."
- It can be a call to action "Now you know what the organisation is aiming to achieve, we want to see you all..."

Each of those statements can be elaborated on to pull together your presentation. However, don't be tempted to elaborate too long. If you're not comfortable with how long it's taking to close the audience probably won't be either!

Once you signal that the end is coming, people start fidgeting if you don't get there fairly promptly. Time your close. In a presentation that is more than 30 minutes you can probably get away with up to five minutes. In a shorter presentation the close should be correspondingly shorter.

You should know exactly how long your close is so that, if the time schedule is altered and your 40 minute presentation is cut to 25, you know that you must keep five minutes for the end – if that's how long your end is. Don't cut your ending – the cuts will take place in the main part of your presentation (which we'll come to soon).

FIVE SIMPLE TIPS TO HELP YOU CLOSE WELL

1. Don't be too long–winded in closing – the audience will realise you have nearly finished and may switch off.
2. Do finish on time. This is crucial to a professional speech.
3. Resist the temptation to over emphasise the point at the close – remember "Less is More"
4. A call to action – if you want something to happen, this is the time to ask!
5. Always say "Thank you!"

The Third Tool is to be able to *close effectively*. Practise what to say and how to say it so that you leave a strong message with your audience.

TOOL 4 – Open

*"The secret of getting ahead is getting **started**. The secret of getting **started** is breaking your complex overwhelming tasks into small manageable tasks, and then **starting** on the first one."*

Mark Twain

Let's say your close takes five minutes. What's the logical next thing to do?

If you're going to make a point and finish on it, it probably makes sense that you open and explain what you're going to do.

"Ladies and gentlemen, today I'm here to talk to you about the wonderful collection for our charity and to thank you for all your efforts at the quiz night!"

Not necessarily fancy words – but they will work because they are normal.

It's very simple:

- You know *Why*
- You know the *Point* you wish to make
- You know how to *Close* the speech

So the next step is how to start… or *Open*

Given that this is the point where you first come into direct contact with your audience it's really important that you make an impact.

You know what they say:

> You never get a second chance to make a first impression!

So this part of your presentation is really important – if you catch the audience's attention at this point, the rest will, as they say, be all downhill. If you fail to engage them at the beginning, the rest will be an uphill struggle.

The problem is that your nerves are likely to be at their peak at the point where you start your presentation. Nerves have a number of negative effects – and some positive ones!

Firstly, let's get the basic bit over. Nerves seem to have the effect of putting pressure on your bladder – so 'go' before you go on! Just make sure you are *not* wearing a microphone when you go – or be very, very certain it's turned off. You would be surprised as how often that pre–presentation visit has been broadcast to everyone through a very efficient PA system!

Secondly, nerves can wipe your memory clean. Standing up to speak and suddenly finding that you can't remember a word is quite common too. The simplest remedy is to learn your opening so you can do it in your sleep and have your opening words on a card in your pocket, just in case.

Whatever you decide to use as your approach you need to make sure it is a well–rehearsed paragraph or two that you can recite on automatic pilot!

Practise it until you're word perfect. Practise in the car, in the shower and at any other opportunity. Make sure it introduces your presentation and helps the audience to understand where you'll be going. When you're word perfect, time it – you need to know how long your opening and closing are – once you subtract this time from the total time you've got for your presentation you know how long you can talk in the main part of your presentation.

Thirdly, nerves can tighten your vocal chords. If you've ever heard anyone start to speak in a squeaky voice, then hastily clear their throat and continue in more normal tones, you'll know exactly what I mean.

Athletes warm up before an event, opera singers and actors warm their voices up – so it's a good idea to do a few vocal exercises if you can do them privately, just to ensure you don't sound like a strangled mouse when you open your mouth.

Nerves also have some positive effects.

- A touch of nerves will ensure you don't get complacent and, therefore, you'll give a better presentation.
- Nerves ensure you retain that 'edge'. You'll be sharper and more alert.
- The adrenalin that nerves create will keep you on top of the game!

So, what's the best approach?

- Say why you are there!
- Pose a question
- Start with a relevant story
- Set the scene
- Say something controversial

SAY WHY YOU ARE THERE!

Most audiences don't like to be kept in the dark. To explain what you have come to talk about – and why – is always a good opener.

The old cliché: "Tell 'em what you're going to tell 'em; tell it to them; tell 'em what you told them", usually works quite well.

However, you need to present this in a way that sounds interesting. If you just stand up and say "I'm here to talk about next year's sales targets," it won't get your audience excited.

A different approach might be, "We're aiming to double our sales figures in the next twelve months and I'm going to tell you just how that can be done."

People like to know why you've been chosen to talk to them. Sometimes this is explained in your introduction by someone else, but if not, it's a good way to build rapport with your audience. Use your 'Why me?' to break the ice.

"I was surprised when the Sales Director asked me if I'd make this presentation. However, I guess he wanted to be sure that you got someone who really does understand what it's like out there at the sharp end!"

This type of start can be a great way to make contact with your audience – you're getting on their wavelength. You appear human and may even get a few people to smile – they're on your side!

POSE A QUESTION

This is a great way to get audience participation right at the beginning. Ask a question that requires a response and ask for a show of hands.

You'll need to think of a relevant question that will add value to your presentation. Audiences aren't stupid and they're usually very quick to realise that they are being patronised, so you'd better be asking a question that you can justify. At least you'll need to tell them that you'll come back to it as your presentation progresses – and *make sure you do*!

What sort of questions work well?

- How many of you have experienced X? *This engages the audience in the process, they start thinking about their own experience in relation to what you'll be talking about.*
- All those who think it's possible to double our sales figures in the next twelve months please raise your hands. *This requires them to have a clear opinion and to commit to it. It also opens the door for you to ask people why they think that.*
- We're going to be talking about the sales targets for the last year and the next one. What would you prefer – the figures or the graphs? *This is asking them to be involved in shaping the progress of your presentation. Obviously, you will have both prepared and may need to present both, but you should find it easy to focus on the preferred response more than the other. Of course, you'll have people on both sides of the fence so you will need to address their needs as well – and can use this as a device for ensuring you cover everything!*

START WITH A RELEVANT STORY

This is my personal favourite – people love stories. They remember stories long after the data has disappeared from their memories! Starting with a good story is an ideal way to get the audience sitting up and paying attention.

Of course, the story must relate to your presentation, but you should find it easy to find something that explains an element of your key message. You can even tell the story of how you came to be making the presentation – or the story of why you have decided to make this presentation.

Remember how people respond to "Once upon a time..."? Always tell them you're going to tell them a story so they know what to expect.

"I'd like to start by telling you a story."

"Before I start, I'd like to explain just how this presentation came about."

"I'd like to share an experience with you..."

People take things on board better when they know what is coming.

SET THE SCENE

This is a variation on story telling. You'll be asking your audience to use their imagination. It's a sure–fire way to get them involved in the presentation if you do a good job.

You need to think of how you'd describe the situation you're aiming to achieve by your presentation. Now you have to get your audience to visualise the situation that you're going to start from.

For a father of the bride speech it might go something like this:

"Imagine you're sitting at home reading a newspaper. Your eldest daughter walks through the door and says, "Dad, I've got something to tell you."

"In that split second what would go through your mind? Well, I can tell you that when Susie said that to me I imagined the worst.

So I was not concentrating as well as I might when she told me that she was planning to get married to Pete. My response was probably not what she was expecting.

"Never mind, sweetheart, I'm sure we can sort something out. Are you sure you want to go ahead with this?"

For the sales team presentation perhaps you might use real memories:

"Cast your mind back to last year. Do you remember we were sitting here looking at our performance for 2004 and planning how we'd exceed those figures by at least 15% in 2005? How do you think we've done – and what sort of figures will be looking back at this time next year?"

You can use the "Imagine you're..." and then describe your own situation to get the audience on your side. It's usually a very effective means of engaging them.

SAY SOMETHING CONTROVERSIAL

There's nothing like a challenging statement to get the audience's attention! As long as you're able to justify it – or disprove it – with the rest of your presentation.

Sales director – "I started this year expecting great things – but I certainly didn't expect the results we got."

Expert – "I thought I knew everything there was to know about my subject. I certainly didn't expect to learn something new from a 12 year old."

Father of the Bride – "The moment I found out Susie planned to marry Pete I knew it would be a disaster."

You get the idea!

Of course, you'll have something to follow these statements up with that makes sense. I'm sure you'll have your own challenges to throw the audience and get them to pay attention.

FIVE SIMPLE TIPS TO HELP YOU OPEN YOUR PRESENTATION

1. Always take a deep breath before you start.
2. Always look up at the audience – let them know you are ready.
3. Wait for the audience to be ready, don't start too quickly.
4. Be patient if an audience isn't settling down.
5. Once you start, keep going – command respect.

So that's Tool Number Four – *Open, get the audience's attention,* make an impact and use one of a range of approaches that makes you feel comfortable.

TOOL 5 – Body

"In the middle of difficulty lies opportunity."
Albert Einstein

So just for arguments sake, let's say your *Close* (your finish, your end, whatever word you like to use), is five minutes and your *Open*, (the way you start your speech) is five minutes, that's ten minutes.

And let's say somebody has invited you to make a twenty–minute speech. That leaves you ten minutes for the Body.

It's not rocket science, is it? But this is what happens in reality:

"Bill, we know we said twenty minutes, but the other speaker has gone over a bit, so you actually have fifteen! OK?"

With most people they'll start the same way (5 minutes), use the same body (10 minutes), but how much time do they have left to finish? Very little!

As a result they rush through the end. Did they get their point over? Did it work for them or the audience? Probably not.

So if you don't trim the close down, what do you do?

We've already established that your opening is the place you make an impact, engage the audience and introduce your subject to they'll understand what's coming.

We've already agreed that you need to start with the end in mind. You need to make your point clearly and concisely.

That leaves the middle – or *Body* – of your presentation. This is the part where you will have to 'prune' some of the material to fit the slot you've got. This applies whether you have advance warning or not.

If you have a presentation that you make more than once, you won't always be able to guarantee you get the same amount of time in which to make it. You might have been given 45 minutes the first time you do the presentation, but the next time it's only

30 minutes. Then later you're asked to fill in a gap somewhere with a 20 minute version.

The Open and Close are still important – and you must have a good middle that provides information and helps you to make your point, *but* the level of detail can vary depending on the time you have.

Here are some things that will help you to overcome this 'variable' Body:

- Have a supermarket approach
- Relax and get into the swing
- Don't stick to one format
- Put everything in – then MASSAGE it!
- Use handouts to give information

Whenever I share the five steps to speaking with an audience I always get the audience to stand up in rows, turn to face the wall and ask them to massage the shoulders of the person in from of them. Then I ask them to reverse and return what they have received!

Some people enjoy this more than others!

However, the purpose is simple; when dealing with the Body of the speech – the bit that is flexible – simply remember to massage the body don't change the start or finish change the bit in the middle!

You may forget my words but you won't forget the action!

HAVE A SUPERMARKET APPROACH

In other words, have more than you need in your basket (the Body) and simply use what you need in the actual time available. This means you need to plan what your main points are – usually between three and five points only.

The next step is to look at what will help you to illustrate what you want to say. This might include a variety of data, facts, anecdotes, stories, examples and so on.

You may need to do some research to make sure you have a variety of different information and also different formats for it – so some verbal, some visual, some participative.

Put together your presentation with everything in it, in the right order, of course.

RELAX AND GET INTO THE SWING

Once you've established what is in your presentation you can relax and get into the swing of things.

You don't have to worry whether you'll make the end in time, but can concentrate on using your anecdotes and information to help the audience to see the same picture that you do.

If you relax your material will come to life. If you're stiff and worried about getting everything in you'll come over that way and it will be much harder to get your audience on your side. You've probably seen it happen yourself – a presenter that is so focused on the presentation that they never connect with the audience.

DON'T STICK TO ONE FORMAT

Firstly, your audience won't concentrate fully for the whole of your presentation. Most people manage about eight minutes before their mind wanders. If you just talk to them, you'll find it hard going. Here's some things that you can do to vary the pace a bit:

- When you're talking use your voice effectively. Use pauses to let people digest a particular point. Alter the pace at which you speak to help to make your point.
- Use PowerPoint to show graphs, diagrams and pictures that will help you to illustrate your points. However, don't use it as a means of having your notes on the screen. Remember that PowerPoint is a visual AID not something to hide behind!
- If you have a short piece of film on video in your PowerPoint presentation, that demonstrates a key point, by all means use that too.

- Get audience participation by asking questions, or getting them to discuss something and then make a yes/no decision and gather their responses. Ask for individual's experiences – and choose one or two to listen to.
- Put key information onto a flip chart – or quotes that demonstrate a particular point.

All these things will help you to keep your audience engaged and prolong their attention to your message.

PUT EVERYTHING IN – THEN *MASSAGE* IT!

When you first start to create the speech put everything in that you have, and then massage it – brutally!

Decide what is essential to your presentation – this is the core of your Body that will always be in your presentation.

Next, look at other elements. What will improve the understanding of your audience, these are the next to leave in, if you've that bit of extra time.

Then you can decide what else you leave in, or cut out, depending on the available time.

This ensures that you don't just run out of time and miss out on making your point in your Close. And stops you running over time and having an audience who all start checking their watches!

USE HANDOUTS TO GIVE INFORMATION

Develop a handout that has ALL your key points on it. You can refer to this in your presentation, "Ladies and Gentleman. A full handout will be made available after the presentation." This will have two benefits, one the audience don't need to take so many notes and, therefore, will concentrate more on what you're saying. Secondly, if you don't have the time to cover everything in detail, they will still get all the information in the notes.

Handouts can have visuals included and can be a combination of headings, bullet points and narrative.

Perhaps, as I do, offer website downloads or weblinks, video emails, conference calls or email follow–up – whatever you think will be helpful to your audience.

Don't make them too cryptic or people won't be able to remember what it was all about. Good handouts are not too long, but cover all the key points.

If there is a lot of information, consider some of it being attached as an appendix. You can also include sources of information, rather than the information itself.

People remember more when they have something to remind them!

FIVE SIMPLE TIPS TO HELP YOU WORK YOUR BODY

1. Don't batter the audience with facts and figures – make your point simply.
2. Don't be the support to the PowerPoint show.
3. Gauge the audience's reception to the body and adjust the close if the feedback is different to what you expected!
4. Vary your pitch and tone to keep interest.
5. Remember an audience's attention span is about eight minutes –so vary things!

So that's Tool Number Five – *craft a Body that gets your message across*, whether it's a short or longer time frame.

Finally, if you use these Tools and really understand them you'll remember the process. That's really important.

The first time I really used the tools we've been talking about was when I was on a trip in America in 1999.

I was asked if I would like to speak to a 'few people' because they had never had anyone come over from England.

I'd never been to America before, as we were driving along they said it was just around the corner, and we drove into a thing called the CNN building. I didn't even know who CNN were! Naïve? YES!

We went in through all these doors, they told me it was quite a big room so they had to stick a microphone on me, which I'd never used before.

And then we walked into the room – several hundred people!

I had the walk from the back of the room to the front to think of what the heck I was going to say. I used the process I have just given you and to this day I have no idea what I said! Everyone said it was natural and I was blessed, I think.

What I am saying is that this process does work and it will help you, please share it!

It's a good common sense structure and although it may obvious, for many people it isn't at all obvious. Well, common sense isn't always that common, is it? Quite often you'll hear speeches where the process isn't being used – and the result isn't there.

So it's important to take time out and think about it. Understand why you are speaking, what's your point, (start with the end in mind), create your close first, then create the start and then work out the bit in the middle.

This process of Why, Point, Close, Open and Body is very simple, very practical, and it works. Think of it as your passport to successful speaking.

FIVE TECHNIQUES

TECHNIQUE 1 – Believe In You!

*"Be **yourself**; everyone else is already taken."*
Oscar Wilde

You need to be focused on believing you can give your audience something of value – not focused on your nerves! This means that you need to turn up for the start of the speech. Not only in person, but in your head as well. Be ready to give them the best you can and you'll find the nerves are a bit less.

Turn up with enthusiasm and passion for your subject and an audience will forgive you a great deal in lack of skill because they can sense your belief – without it even the most technically crafted speech falls flat.

Think about the presentations that you've had to sit through. Aren't the ones that have flown by and left you with something useful usually delivered by people who seem to totally believe in their subject and have enthusiasm for it? Contrast that sort of presentation with the ones you've probably also had to sit through that have been delivered by someone who obviously knows their stuff, but doesn't seem to be excited by it. I'm sure you'll remember the presentation was dry, flat and not particularly memorable as far as actual content was concerned.

So use tools to make sure you're fit to deliver your stuff. I find visualising the audience applauding at the end and smiling at me works well for me. Visualisation is a powerful technique and can affect you positively or negatively.

Just think about the difference between:

- An audience clapping enthusiastically, on their feet, smiling and looking really excited at the end of your presentation.
- A polite smattering of applause, quickly over, and people looking to see who's on next.

If you *knew* that the result was going to one of these two how would this affect your presentation?

I know that if I thought I was only going to get lukewarm appreciation at the end, I'd rush through my presentation and want to get off. Would that ensure that I got the result I was expecting?

Of course it would!

So you need to think about that enthusiastic audience – because, if that's what you're expecting you're going to give it your very best shot and it will show. Of course, you'll get that really positive reception – because you'll deserve it!

TECHNIQUE 2 – For The Audience

*"Of **audiences**: they were really tough – they used to tie their tomatoes on the end of a yo–yo, so they could hit you twice."*
Bob Hope

What do I mean 'for the audience'?

Well it's very easy, especially if you're doing a lot of speaking, to slip into the 'I'm a speaker' mode. I hope you get over that very quickly, but this might help.

I always want to share something that you can take away and use practically and immediately from the speech. My role in life, when I stand in front of you to speak, is to give you something that will make a difference. It's not to say look at me, how good am I?

Here are some very quick figures that are remarkably accurate with the majority of audiences with more than ten people:

1. 10% of an audience this size like to know where they're going, so you need to ask their permission straight away.

   "I'm going to cover five steps to speaking, is that OK with you?"

   Most people's heads will nod and they will have made the decision that they wanted to listen. If you get an audience to say 'yes, that's ok' 10% are probably onside with you, so you've got a good start.

2. 30% of the audience just want to have a bit of fun along the way. They don't want to sit there bored to tears. I hope that, as you've followed all we've been covering you'll have found a way to add a bit of humour and fun to your presentation.

   If you've brought those people along, you now have 40% of the audience who are now with you.

3. 35% of the audience simple want to know how much you care. Forget about all the technical stuff, I want to see how

much you care about what you're talking about, why you're talking about it and that you're a caring individual. Personally, I tell stories about my family to show you that I really believe in what I'm saying. We've got 75% of the audience with us now.

4. 25% left if the sums add up, and if they don't, that 25% are going to tell me immediately because they want structure, they want form. If you've used the formats we've covered so far, you'll have given them that. That's 100%!

TECHNIQUE 3 – Build A Relationship

"There are three things to aim at in public speaking: first, to get into your subject, then to get your subject into yourself, and lastly, to get your subject into the heart of your ***audience****."*
Alexander Gregg

Remember in my introduction about the group purchasing director who said that 90% of individuals and organizations fail to make a long lasting relationship and don't get the business?

That's nine out of ten sales pitches fail!

Let me tell you a story:

The Biscuit Kid

I was in my late twenties and had finally got the opportunity to get my first real sales job with my own patch, car and everything! Boy, was I excited. I was told that I would have extensive training over some months, the company would walk with me every step of the way and that I wasn't expected to make a real contribution until my second year...

After two days head office training (this was a major Financial Services Organisation) I was sent to the branch to meet my branch manager.

I entered his office, he looked over his glasses and said, "Every new sales person brings in twelve major accounts in their first year, here's the keys to your car, now clear off and sell!" (He didn't use the words 'clear off' by the way!)

Welcome to real life!

So for the next three months I spoke to anyone who would stand still long enough and one morning I was making a coffee in the office, when the wise old hand of the branch (we'll call him Bill) said, "let's take five minutes. So how are you doing?"

It was at this point I had to admit that I was not doing well at all. In fact, with more children on the way the pressure was on.

"Bill, I am dying out there," I said.

He looked at me and said, "Do you have one clear target you know you could help – given the chance?"

"Absolutely." I can see it to this day – a motor dealer forecourt, the right sort of prospect at that time.

"Well, I suggest you take a pack of biscuits with you and share a cup of coffee."

He stared at me intently and said, "It never fails!"

With that he went on his way...

So that afternoon I went armed with biscuits (my favourite, of course) and as I went onto the forecourt I saw the owner, Fred.

Fred looked at me, stretched his hand out in a stop pose and said, "Son, I know who you are and where you're from and when I need some help, I'll call you. I haven't time to talk to you today, I'm too busy."

Dejected, I turned heel and started to walk away when I got angry and shouted, "Fred, what's your favourite biscuits?"

"You what?" he said.

"Fred what's your favourite biscuits?" I said with conviction. (Remember, "It never fails!")

"'Obnobs."

"When do you have your first cup of tea in the morning Fred?"

"6.30am crack of sparrows," he said.

"Good, I'll bring the biscuits and I'll see you in the morning at 6.30am – I'm busy now so I'll talk to you then."

And I walked off the forecourt with Fred's jaw on the ground!

So next morning at 6.30am Fred lifts the shutters to the premises. "Good Morning Fred, get the kettle on!"

It was me, grinning, clutching a pack of 'Obnobs and I walked straight past him into the office – and he let me!

To this day I have never asked him what he thought and I sincerely believe he was so surprised to see this cheeky kid that he didn't know what to do!

Six weeks later I had my first major account!

Fast forward to the monthly character assassination meeting – oops, I mean the monthly sales meeting!

There were a number of us around the table and the manager stopped his tirade of why we were performing poorly, took his glasses off and looked straight at me...

"Peter, well done your first major account –how did you do it?"

Not only was I young, but also naïve.

I related the story to a hushed room and finished with "Well you can see it wasn't me really, it was all Bill's idea – the biscuit trick worked!"

I turned to Bill specifically and continued, "So it was all down to you Bill, you really helped me, thank you so much..."

All eyes in the room turned to Bill.

"Bill, the biscuit trick?"

Bill went all colours of the rainbow and said, "Well I had to tell the kid something – I've never tried it like that before!"

At that second I realised a few home truths!

No one did twelve new major accounts per year – in fact, if you did one it was lucky!

? That I had been very naïve.

? There was more to sales than I first thought.

? That I couldn't stand 'Obnobs!

Well the joke was on them and I was excited so much that I went to the local supermarket and bought a carton of "'Obnobs" and attacked the other major accounts I had identified.

Guess what?

It was never quite the same, because I suspect I didn't have the blind faith that I had before. However the results are worth knowing.

I signed two further accounts that year (I became Sales Person of the Year).

Three others were never going to change suppliers but were always willing to chat.

Three just stole my biscuits (well it was the Motor Trade).

And here's the most surprising, three said, "You're trying to bribe me to go away and don't come back!"

To this day I cannot understand that viewpoint, but it made me think long and hard and the conclusions I came to are simply this:

80% of sales are simply hard work persistence and enthusiasm, as in all business.

20% of sales is the ability to create a relationship, but it's the difference between winning and losing and is therefore the most critical part.

No relationship – No sale.

It took me a long time to understand that I could do business with most people once I understood where they were coming from as opposed to to what I wanted...

This made my career improve dramatically.

To close a sale you need to see the world through your client's eyes not just your own and in a manner that you both feel comfortable with – and if you can help them – then, perhaps, you will also get what you want!

So what's the point of the story?

It's exactly the same for any speech. When you're speaking it's just like closing the sale. So see the audience through their eyes – and make a successful speech!

TECHNIQUE 4 – Know Your Lines

*"I had butterflies in my stomach. I don't **know** why I was so nervous–maybe because I don't **know** how to pronounce half the **lines** I have to say today. They're in some made–up language."*
Alyson Hannigan

There are a few people who are confident speakers. They're happy to stand up and talk on any occasion, but some of them don't think they need to prepare in advance, they just stand up and talk, in the same way that they talk to the person sat next to them at a meeting.

I always felt reasonably confident getting up to speak, although I would usually do a bit of planning before I actually got on my feet. Until this happened.

A little while ago I was at my local breakfast networking club and the President asked if I would appear with a friend of mine later in the year to take a master class in speaking. Immediately I said, "Yes!"

She said, "Great it's in three months time," and I said, "Good that's plenty of time to prepare..."

Now my friend is twenty–eight years a professional actor, director, author and producer and when I said we were going to do a double act he said, "Great! When?"

I said what I had agreed with the President.

"Oh my God!" he said, "We've only got three months!"

His nickname for me is the 'Winger' because in business we have a tendency to 'wing' things, as client needs dictate – it goes with the territory.

Of course my nickname for him is 'Luvvy' as you would probably expect for his profession!

He is an all round good guy and rarely gets upset – however this was one of those occasions.

"Peter, you just don't get it do you!" he said.

Taken aback I said, "Calm down mate, what's the matter?"

He said, "Look, let's explain this to you in a different way," (he must have read this book!)

"You and Anny (my wife) went to the theatre in London recently didn't you?"

"Yes," I said, "cost me an arm and a leg, but it was worth it and we had a great time."

"The tickets for the theatre were good value then?" he asked quietly.

"Yes," I said, still not understanding.

"Did you expect the actors to know their lines, Peter?"

"Too right at that money!" I said.

There was a long silence and he said again

"Did you expect the actors to know their lines, Peter?" This time more forcefully.

Then it finally hit me – he probably wanted to use a sledgehammer!

Either in business or when we really have something personal to say, how often do we take the time to know our lines?

Most of us simply put things off until the last moment, 'wing' things and make statements like "thank God that's over!" instead of preparing by using a simple, well–proven process that will make our impact so much greater. Even when the pressure can be huge we still delay – ask any Dad just prior to his speech at his daughter's wedding.

Yet the answers to overcoming our number one fear are so simple, the process so straightforward – if we take the time and trouble to use them.

Please, wherever possible, don't be a 'Winger'

Use the ideas in this book, practise, know your lines, be courageous and be yourself.

And you will stand out in front of any audience...

And your message will have a powerful impact ...

And you will be the individual who stands head and shoulders above the rest – perhaps, not someone who is perfect – but someone who clearly knows their craft...

TECHNIQUE 5 – Speaking Effectively

"Beautifully crafted words have the power to captivate the mind of anybody. A sweet–tongued man or woman is loved by one and all. An Audience is always attracted towards those who can ***speak*** *efficiently and* ***effectively****."*

Sam Verda

Speaking effectively for me is summed up by one story – another personal one.

It's 1am in the morning. Sara is very upset and has been crying. It's the night before her first GCSE exams and she's struggling – nothing is going in. She's bright, intelligent and has done her homework, but the pressure is getting to her, she just can't see the words on the paper.

Downstairs is Dad, he looks up and thinks, "Sara's light is still on, doesn't she realise she has an exam in the morning? Better I go see what the problem is."

He goes upstairs. Sara is sitting on her bed, looking at her father for some comfort and advice.

What would you say?

"What's the problem?"

"How can I help you?"

Perhaps gave her a hug?

He says, "Don't be so bloody silly, don't you realise you have an exam in the morning, turn your light off and get to sleep!"

She gave him the look that only a woman can give a man – the look of 'you will wither and perish in hell!'

He looks at her and thinks 'Uh oh.'

Did she turn the light off? No!

Did he get what he wanted? No!

Did she stay upset? Doubly.

What did he do?

Turned around and said, "Bloody kids! They don't do anything I want them to do..." and went downstairs.

Did he go to sleep? No!

Next morning he thought, 'I blew that. It's her exams and it's important. How can I help her?'

There is a saying, "When the pupil is ready the teacher will appear."

Somebody lent him a tape made by a doctor who had four teenage daughters. There were some different ideas about how to get on with each other, based on personality. Good practical sound stuff, not mumbo jumbo. So, when she got home that evening, he'd listened to it, and thought, "I'll try it. I'll try anything to help."

So he said to her, "Sara, you can be in charge, you can be in control, but when 11pm comes, I'd like you to turn out your light and go to sleep."

She said, "Yeah, OK."

For the rest of the evening he was thinking, "What a waste of time, this won't work" Yet at 11pm she got up from her desk, walked up the stairs, shut her door and turned her light off, with her dad thinking, "How did that happen?"

He thought, "I'll try some more of this stuff!"

Dad started getting more involved, just to help, playing the tape in the car with the family listening, because they all wanted to help Sara get through a tough time.

One morning they're driving along listening to the tape. It was funny and entertaining too, which was even better. Then a voice piped up, "Didn't you say that to me this morning?" It was Sara!

Silence and embarrassment in the car. “Yes, well actually, love, we’ve been using this to help and er – look, we just wanted to help.”

Sara goes quiet for the longest five minutes of her life and says, “This stuff is really good. You should learn more about it”.”

So I did – because Sara is my elder daughter – if you hadn’t already guessed!

That’s what made me go to America to learn more about personality. I was taught one thing, it’s a powerful phrase that’s changed my personal life, my family life, and my business life, and that is:

‘You need to learn to say the same thing – but in a different way!’

It’s an old phrase, you may have heard it before, but the point is, I hadn’t heard it. I knew it, but I hadn’t heard it. More, importantly, I wasn’t using it.

When I said, “Sara, you can be in charge, you can be in control, but when 11pm comes, I’d like you to turn out your light and go to sleep.” For the first time in my life, instead of looking through my eyes, I took my glasses my off and looked at the world through my daughter’s eyes. I spoke to her in language she was more comfortable with and it had an effect. It made a major difference.

Why am I sharing this with you and what has it got to do with speaking?

Everything!

To me speaking or presenting to any audience is about the ability to share your thoughts and ideas in away that each individual can digest, understand and, hopefully, agree with.

It’s about putting yourself into their shoes not your own.

Seeing life in a way they see and understand, and not taking the process for granted.

It's also understanding that you may not get it right every time and that, on any given day, you cannot touch everyone in the audience. That it's OK, it's just not for them at that time.

And maybe there will be another time another place or perhaps another speaker that can get the message to them!

THE NATURAL SPEAKER

I have often been told that I make speaking in front of (especially large) audiences seem very easy and relaxed. People sometimes think that, perhaps, I don't understand what the fear is really like.

A twelve–year–old boy was standing in front of an English class about to read a poem. He was at a school which really didn't suit him – an engineering school his proud Dad had worked nights for many years to get the extra money necessary for his son to attend – unfortunately the boy wasn't skilled in mechanical areas in fact the one thing he could do was to be the boy who would stand and read out aloud – the one place he could shine.

He read the poem out to the class....

The Tyger by William Blake

Tyger, Tyger, burning bright,
In the forest of the night,
What immortal hand or eye
Could frame thy fearful symmetry?

In what distant deeps or skies
Burnt the fire of thine eyes?
On what wings dare he aspire?
What the hand dare seize the fire?

And what shoulder, and what art,
Could twist the sinews of thy heart?
When thy heart began to beat,
What dread hand forged thy dread feet?

What the hammer? What the chain?
In what furnace was thy brain?
What the anvil? What dread grasp
Dared its deadly terrors clasp?

When the stars threw down their spears
And watered heaven with their tears,
Did He smile his work to see?
Did He who made the lamb make thee?

Tyger, Tyger, burning bright,
In the forest of the night,
What immortal hand or eye
Dare frame thy fearful symmetry?

The boy looked at the English teacher – they both disliked each other intensely

"What does the poem mean, boy?"

"It's about a Tiger, sir."

"Roper, you are an ignorant cretin with a Birmingham accent. Sit down and never stand up in this school again."

So, I didn't. In fact, for ten years I never stood up to read anything of any description. Then one day, at 22 years of age, I had to read out a ten–minute presentation to an audience of 1000 – yes, 1000 – people at the company I worked for.

When I had finished I realised by the look on the audience's faces that they were simply pleased it hadn't been them. Slowly, but surely, I started to read and present in public – never telling anyone what had happened to me.

So I do understand the fear!

Fast forward thirty odd years – I was speaking at a function in Birmingham and after the event I met an individual, who introduced me to his wife – a head of year for maths at a local school. Wouldn't you know it was my old school! The one I swore I would never set foot in again.

She challenged me to spend a morning with her and I had the chance to stand in that same class room all those years later – and exorcised some demons along the way.

I had the chance to speak at a network marketing organisation event shortly after and to complete the chapter of my life I decided to read the poem as part of a speech about empowerment – as a surprise to my wife, Anny, who was with me that day.

After the event Anny said that she was amazed that I had read the poem, as she knows how much of an effect it had had on my life.

"That's not the half of it!" I said, "I've been practising it in secret for over a week to make sure I could deliver it without getting too emotional."

But here's the rub – when I read it all those years later I realised that the English teacher was right – it's not about a TIGER!

Go back and read about The TYGER again!

Since I have shared this story I have listened to literally hundreds of people tell me their similar stories. Many have thanked me for helping them to get over their fears.

My message to you is simple,

I want you to feel free to speak –
you can be a natural presenter!

"People like People who are natural..."
Peter Roper

Peter Roper

PS... and remember "If I can help you in any way – just let me know!"

Bibliography

Some of these books are mentioned and directly quoted in '...and death came third!'. Others have shaped our thoughts over time or are simply 'essential' further reading on networking or presentation skills. There are many good business books out there, these are some of our favourites surrounding these topics. If you would like to recommend any other books to us, please do get in touch.

Bob Burg, *Endless Referrals*, McGraw–Hill, 2005, 0071462074
Carol Harris, *Networking for Success*, Oak Tree Press, 2000, 1860761615
Dale Carnegie, *How to Win Friends and Influence People*, Vermilion, 2006, 0091906814
Dale Spender, *Man Made Language*, Rivers Oram Press, 1998, 0863584012
Ivan Misner, Don Morgan, *Masters of Networking*, Bard Press, 2000, 1885167482
James Surowiecki, *The Wisdom of Crowds*, Abacus, 2005, 0349116059
Jan Vermieren, *Let's Connect*, Step by Step, 2006, 9054668865
Jeffrey Mayer, *Creating Opportunities by Networking*, (eBook) Succeeding in Business, 2002, 3129444184
Jerry R Wilson, *Word of Mouth Marketing*, John Wiley & Sons, 1994, 0471008583
John Gray, *Men are from Mars, Women are from Venus*, Harper Collins, 2002, 0007152590
Julia Hubbel, *The Art of Principled Networking: When you Schmooze, You Lose*, (eBook), www.principlednetworking.com
Leil Lowndes, *How to Talk to Anyone*, Contemporary Books, 2003, 007141858X
Lesley Everett, *Walking Tall*, Lesley Everett, 2004, 0954893506
Malcolm Gladwell, The Tipping Point, Abacus, 2002, 0349113467
Mike Southon, Chris West, *The Beermat Entrepreneur*, Prentice Hall, 2006, 0273704540
Nigel Risner, *You Had Me at 'Hello'*, Forest Oak, 2003, 0954360028
Peter Thomson, *Speak Up*, (Audio Programme), PTI International, 2001
Robert Cialdini, *Influence: Psychology of Persuasion*, William Morrow, 1999, 0688128165
Robert Rohm, *Positive Personality Profiles*, Voyager Press, 1994, 0964108003
Roy Sheppard, *Rapid Result Referrals*, Centre Publishing, 2001, 1901534049

Shad Helmstetter, *What to Say when you Talk to Yourself*, Pocket Books, 1990, 0671708821
Stephen Covey, *The Seven Habits of Highly Successful People*, Free Press, 2004, 0743272455
Susan RoAne, *How to Work a Room*, Harper Collins, 2000, 0060957859
Ted Nicholas, *Magic Words that Bring you Riches*, Access Publishers Network, 1999, 1887741003
Timothy I Templeman, *The Referral of a Lifetime*, Berrett–Koehler, 2005, 1576753212

About The Authors

Andy Lopata

Andy Lopata lives and breathes business–to–business networking. He is the Managing Director of Business Referral Exchange Networking (BRE), one of the UK's largest referral focused networking companies and has developed a series of successful tips and tools for building networks and referral based marketing strategies.

He offers a refreshing new insight into networking opportunities. His approach concentrates on the capability to listen, to inform others what you do and to recognise opportunities that could be of mutual benefit. Using his techniques, many of his clients have reported that they have produced previously untapped business, previously missed out on for some time.

By getting business managers to change the way they regard their clients, their associates and themselves, Andy's methods have consistently produced new ideas and clearer focus for businesses. These have resulted in increased sales and buyer satisfaction.

Fear of approaching strangers is often the main reason why people find it hard to network. Andy believes that everyone has a value to someone and believes that there are strategies we can all learn to quickly overcome fear and build better and deeper relationships.

The tips and tools he provides have helped many of his clients including; Barclays Bank, British International Franchise Exhibition, Business Link, Chamber of Commerce, Chartered Institute of Management Accountants, Institute of Management, Interalliance plc, Intellect (Intellect is the trade body for the UK based information technology, telecommunications and electronics industry), KallKwik, Pitman Training, TaxAssist Direct and WSI Internet.

Andy is the co-author of the 2005 book 'Building a Business on Bacon and Eggs' (Life Publications) and has also produced a popular networking tips booklet 'It's Not Rocket Science' and co-produced a networking CD 'It's Not What You Know' with the sales trainer Keith Banfield.

Peter Roper

Peter Roper is known as 'The Natural Presenter', he is a co–founder of Guruonline and its Lead Presenter.

In 1996 Peter left corporate life after a highly successful corporate career spanning three decades including a four time 'Sales Representative of the Year Award' with two different organisations. He established his highly successful "Natural Partnership" – Inspiring individuals and organisations to create NATURAL ADVANTAGE and growth through five key strategies; Natural Brand; Natural Relationships; Natural Influence; Natural Presentation; and Natural Business Growth.

In 2004 Peter made 153 speeches and presentations inspiring individuals and organisations to grow naturally. As "The Natural Presenter" he is recognised as the UK's highly visible expert on being Natural – particularly when speaking and presenting. He has spoken to over 150,000 people in the last six years.

Peter is Immediate Past President and a fellow of the Midlands Chapter of the Professional Speakers Association (PSA). He is also the first recipient of the "Significant Achievement" award presented by Personality Insights Inc. Atlanta USA in 2000.

He has been Chairman for the past four years of the 'Sales Executive of the Year Award', for the MARCHE Awards For Excellence and a Senior Consultant for PTI the leading UK consultancy for Business Growth. Peter is an advisor for AIESEC the world's largest student organisation, an international platform for young people to discover and develop their potential.

Peter is author of the acclaimed book 'Feel Free To Speak' and includes in his client list: Business Referral Exchange, Business Over Breakfast, BFB, MARCHE, The Institute of Directors, Meeting Planners International (MPI), the Professional Speakers Association, The Women's Institute (W.I.), Barclays Bank, HSBC Bank, Lloyds TSB, National Westminster Bank, The Royal Bank of Scotland, Practical Rental, Renault Trucks, United Rental, Prontaprint!, Anglia Telecoms, American Golf, Marriott Hotel Group, Westons Cider Group, Hereford County Council, numerous charities, ADSIS, AIESEC, Academy of Chief Executives, Academy of High Achievers, Action International, IMS, breakfast clubs, networking clubs, Accountant groups, Solicitor groups, Young Professional groups plus many, many more.

So, You Want To Know More...?

Please visit our website www.deathcamethird.com where we will be providing you with lots of free 'stuff', including articles on networking and presentations, details of our speaking engagements and useful links to organisations such as Business Referral Exchange, the Professional Speakers Association and others who can help you with your networking or your speaking.

Please also feel free to contact us with your thoughts on the book, your stories or your questions. Naturally, we'd also be delighted to hear from you if you'd like either or both of us to speak for your organisation.

Andy Lopata – andy@brenet.co.uk

Peter Roper – peter@peterroper.com

Download your FREE 'Killer Business Card' guide

The average business card gets looked at 3 times...

That's more than many adverts and typically a lot more than any direct mail you could send. The humble business card is perhaps one of your most effective pieces of marketing literature if used correctly.

Unfortunately, many of us just don't have a clue what needs to go on a business card to make it into a *killer* business card... but you're going to find out!

Your business card is more than just an essential piece of stationery. It is actually one of the most efficient, elegant and powerful sales and marketing tools – apart from yourself – you'll ever possess.

So you owe it to yourself to make it count!

This FREE nitty-gritty guide, will give you everything you need to know to create business cards that will help you get even more success from your networking efforts – whether you've designed a thing in your life before or not.

www.deathcamethird.com/killer